Knockin' on Heaven's Door

Knockin' on Heaven's Door

A True Story of Courage and Sacrifice

Don Busi

Knockin' on Heaven's Door
A True Story of Courage and Sacrifice

Copyright 2013 by Donald J. Busi
2nd Edition
Copyright 2008
1st Edition

All rights reserved. No part of this book may be used or reproduced by any means, graphic electronic, or mechanical, including photocopying, recording, taping or by any information storage system without the written permission of the author except in the case of brief quotations embodied in critical articles and reviews.

Because of the nature of the Internet, any web addresses or links contained in this book may have changed since the publication and may no longer be valid.

This book may be ordered through booksellers or by contacting the author at:
Don Busi
868 Abaco Path
The Villages, FL. 32163
303-521-0351

ISBN: 978-0615732497
ISBN:: 0615732497

Printed in the United States of America

For my father Joe, the most courageous man I've ever known!

Contents

Introduction 7

Chapter 1 10
Mayhem, Death and Destruction
June 6, 1944 – D-Day – 0730 Hours - Second Wave

Chapter 2 29
No Day of Rest
June 7th – D-Day Plus One

Chapter 3 34
Hedgerow Hell and the Silver Star
June 9th – July 10th

Chapter 4 49
Rattled Nerves
July 11th – Hill 192 – St. Lo, France

Chapter 5 52
Snipers
July 21st - August 7th

Chapter 6 65
The Messerschmitt and the Bronze Star
August 8th – 16th

Chapter 7 70
Fifteen Minutes of Fame
August 25th

Chapter 8 75
First Squad Annihilated
August 26th - A Horrible Day

Chapter 9 80
Unbelievable Luck
August 28th – September 19th – Brest, France

Chapter 10 87
Ah! Gay Paris
September 26th – October 4th – Paris

Chapter 11 90
Thick Forest and Nowhere to Hide
October 4th – December 16th – Hurtgen Forest, Belgium

Chapter 12 104
Death Awaits Them All
December 16th – 19th - Battle of the Bulge
Lausdell Crossroads - Rocherath, Belgium

Chapter 13 141
V.E. Day and the Long Road Home
April 6th – June 23rd, 1945

Chapter 14 144
The Doughboy Returns
May 2nd – 5th, 2005 - Normandy, France

Chapter 15 155
Pomp, Circumstance and One Bad Memory
May 12th – 16th, 2005 – Luxembourg & Belgium

Afterword 160

References 163

Glossary 164

Introduction

For over forty-five years I have heard the stories. They didn't seem real when I was younger, but as I grew older they became extremely interesting.

My father's stories of his World War II experience told of heroics and courage that many people only read about or see in movies, yet I had been listening to them since I was eight years old. Always listening intently, I heard the words but never really understood or appreciated what had actually happened to this man during those dreadful months and years of World War II.

Eighty-six years old as of this writing, Sergeant Joseph Busi's life began in the back woods of Western Pennsylvania in abject poverty. To quote a friend: "He wasn't poor, he was PO!" Nine brothers and sisters, mom, dad and uncle lived in a three-room shack with little to eat and even less hope for the future. His Italian immigrant father worked sixteen-hour days in the local coalmine and Joe was lucky to finish the eighth grade. His father died in 1937, just seventeen years after Joe was born, at the height of the Depression.

While the entire country suffered through the Depression, Joe's family was so poor they didn't realize that there was a Depression. Things could not have been any worse for the Busi family. Joe worked for a local contractor at age seventeen cutting timber for the local coalmine and when he turned eighteen he began working in the same mine that had enslaved his father (and many more of his brothers as time went by). Four years later on September 19, 1942 something happened to him that would change his life forever…he was inducted into the United States Army in Apollo, Pennsylvania.

On October 8, 1943 just fourteen months after being inducted, he was on his way to Armaugh, Northern Ireland. On June 6, 1944 just eight months later he would embark on a journey that began with the greatest amphibious assault in human history. A day that was, as he described it, "one of the worst days of my life."

The only thing was, that for Sergeant Busi, there would be many more days to come that would be even worse, if that were possible. The fact that he survived D-Day (no small feat) only meant that he would now have to endure six more long months of misery, mayhem and fear that was beyond belief.

His lack of formal education certainly did not affect his ability to be one of the great soldiers to come out of this historic war. His acts of bravery and courage earned him a Bronze Star, a Bronze Oak Leaf Cluster, a Silver Star and a Purple Heart. His cunning and the ability to survive in such brutal conditions may have had its roots in the very poverty in which he grew up. He once told me that he and his siblings grew up "like wild animals." This may have had something to do with his ability to outsmart his enemy and his instincts to stay alive. As you will see though, as good as those instincts and his Army training were, there was a tremendous amount of lady luck involved in his survival.

Some of the stories you are about to read will leave you in disbelief. Many of his commanding officers and soldiers who fought along side him were awe struck by his acts of bravery. These actions not only saved many American lives, but also wreaked immense havoc on the Nazis. He was trained to kill the enemy and he did his job well. If you ask him about his bravery under fire he responds like the rest of the hardened and humble veterans of his generation: "We were just doing the job we needed to do to get back home!"

Although sickened by the death and brutality of war that surrounded him, he continued to fight every day as if it were his last…one battle after another until the final Nazi spearhead at the Battle of the Bulge in the Ardennes. Wounded, bloody and unable to move another step, his only hope was that his death would be quick…yet he lived to tell his story sixty-one years later. How he overcame the incredible odds against his survival is as amazing as the man himself.

In May of 2005 Sergeant Joseph Busi and his family returned to Europe sixty-one years after this incredible event to retrace the steps of his journey. After seeing the places he had been and the description of what happened there, I was inspired to write his story. It is a story of incredible bravery, courage, sacrifice and the will to survive. It is a story about an ordinary man who did extraordinary things. A man who belongs to a group of people that Tom Brokaw describes as "The Greatest Generation." It is a story that needs to be told.

Sergeant Joseph Busi – Second Squad – Company D – Ninth Infantry Regiment – Second Infantry Division – First Army.

Sergeant Joseph Busi –1945
Photo courtesy of Sergeant Joseph Busi

Chapter 1
Mayhem, Death and Destruction
June 6, 1944 – D-Day – 0730 Hours
Second Wave

"Everything they told us that was supposed to happen that day didn't. It was total chaos and all I could see were dead bodies and body parts everywhere. I had never seen anything like it. I just tried to stay alive." -Sergeant Joseph Busi, 2005 interview

U.S. Army Ranger Colonel James Rudder's signal never came. Rudder was assigned to lead three companies of Army Rangers on an assault of a jetty on a beach between Omaha and Utah Beaches. The tidal current and a barrage of German gunfire delayed Rudder's assault by forty minutes. The Allied Naval barrage that preceded him was long over and the Germans had time to regroup before Rudder hit the beach. Unfortunately, he ended up at Point du Hoc where the heavily fortified one hundred-foot cliff presented a daunting task for him and his Rangers.

When Rudder's landing and subsequent success at taking the beach was completed, he was to signal a five hundred man backup team that had been waiting on allied ships offshore. The signal flare never came and believing that the assault had failed U.S. Commanders decided that the five hundred man backup team would be diverted to Omaha beach.

Private Joseph Busi was assigned to the Second Infantry Division, that wasn't scheduled to land at Omaha Beach until June 7th, D-Day + one. Busi's Commanding Officer, Captain Hancock convinced him to take a condensed version of the U.S. Army Ranger training while in Northern Ireland several months prior to the invasion. This got him bumped up to prime time and he became part of the five hundred man backup team to Colonel Rudder on June 6th. And so, just for this one lucky day he was attached to the First Infantry Division.

Also while he was in Northern Ireland, the U.S. Army had designed a special coating that was fixed around the engines of the American Jeeps and trucks that were scheduled to land shortly after the troops on D-Day. This coating was to protect the engines from the seawater as they moved through the shallows on the beach. Busi's job, as well as the other specially trained rangers, was to make sure that this coating was removed as soon as the trucks and the Jeeps hit the sand. This special training also got him bumped up to a front row seat on June 6th. Although he had worried about the problems associated with this seemingly mindless task, he would soon realize that his primary goal on this day would be keeping his head attached to his shoulders.

Joe was a relatively small man; five-foot nine inches tall and he weighed nearly one hundred-seventy pounds. He was very fit and extremely strong from years of hard labor in the Pennsylvania coalmine he left behind. His fitness and strength made him as tough as nails and he had proven his ability to fight in basic training. There wasn't a man in his outfit that would dare pick a fight with him. They all quickly discovered that his small stature was no indication of his toughness.

As he climbed down the rope ladder, the ship that had taken him across the English Channel, just a few hours earlier began to dip and rise violently from the swales of the high seas making it almost impossible to make a smooth transition into the Higgins landing barge.

The Higgins Boat was the special open top barge invented to bring troops ashore. It had a metal-hinged ramp in the front that would open as soon as the flat bottom boat hit the sand…or whatever else was lurking below the surface (it looked like a shoebox without a top and could carry between twenty and thirty men). Just as he was about to board the barge he heard and felt a huge explosion.

The ship adjacent to his, not more than fifty yards away, took a direct hit from the German artillery pounding the Allied ships from their bunkers on shore. The barge shook, water surged in and it rocked violently from side to side. The explosion shook him and rattled his entire body, knocking him off the last few feet of the rope ladder and onto his back to the bottom of the barge. Several other GIs already on the barge also fell as it rolled violently. He scrambled to his feet and crouched low to avoid being hit by shrapnel. At first he thought the very ship he was on had been hit, but he could see the smoke and flames from the adjacent ship. He hadn't been in combat more than fifteen minutes and already he was shocked by what he had just seen. Smoke rose from mid-ship with huge flames, so close he could hear the screams from the poor GIs who hadn't even made it to the Higgins boat. This was as bad as it got, but he still had no idea what was to come.

The barge quickly turned from the ship, moved away and began toward the beach. Dog Red was their landing spot.

American intelligence had reported to the Allied Commanders, as late as May 1944, that the beaches at Normandy were not heavily fortified and the enemy soldiers holding the beaches were mostly P.O.W.s from occupied Nazi territories with few regular army German Soldiers. The Allied Commanders thought that when the huge armada arrived with thousands of allied troops hitting the beaches, shooting at these slackers, the poorly trained and unmotivated defenders would cower. They were sure that these untrained soldiers would either give up or run screaming into the French countryside.

What the Allies didn't know and what Private Busi was about to find out, was that German General Erwin Rommel had heavily fortified this stretch of French shoreline months before the invasion with many four-foot thick concrete bunkers. His defenses also included battle hardened regular army soldiers of the 352nd German Infantry Division that were relocated from the Russian Front along with eighty-eight millimeter guns, machine gun pill boxes, anti-tank guns, mortars and heavy artillery. The Allies were not in for a walk in the park, especially at Omaha.

As Busi's barge groaned toward Dog Red he began to feel sick to his stomach. The stench of death and the scenes of destruction were just beginning to become all too real. The first wave preceded him by about ninety minutes and it looked as if they had all been totally obliterated. The twenty months of rigorous training prior to this day could never have prepared him for the sights and sounds he was now experiencing. As the Higgins Boat chugged closer to the beach the noise was deafening…shells from German artillery exploded literally yards from his boat shaking the flat-bottomed shoebox from side to side. Machine gun fire from the German bunkers began to spray past his boat and his head as he ducked below the hinged ramp in the up position. The deafening roar of fighter aircraft engines overhead added to, what seemed like, total chaos. As they approached the landing site the noises became so loud that it was impossible for anyone else to speak.

The battle became so intense that he closed his eyes as he tried to stay low. One particular haunting sound that seemed to be more noticeable as he approached the beach was the incessant rattling of the German machine guns dug into the bluffs. It seemed as if they never stopped, never rested. The guns were aimed directly at the Higgins boats as they hit the beach and the constant rattling was unnerving.

He tried desperately to maintain his composure as one GI to his right puked up what was left of breakfast. The puke splattered as it hit the bottom of the boat and covered the tops of Busi's combat boots. No one said a word as they all had other worries. He was positioned toward the front of the boat, so he tried to crouch behind the hinged ramp with two or three rows of men in front of him. The rifle that was slung over his right shoulder was now in both hands with a death grip that turned his knuckles white.

"Holy shit…I'm gonna' die…no way out of this!" He thought to himself.

The boat abruptly stopped and in an instant the hinged ramp dropped open in front of him. Moment of truth…there before him was an incredible sight. Smoke, bodies and body parts floating everywhere, hedgehogs, red sea water and about ten yards ahead …the beach. As the first two rows of GIs ran over the ramp several were hit immediately by machine gun fire and fell lifeless into the ankle high water. Several more men continued to run. Unlike many other barges that day, Private Busi's barge managed to maneuver around the German-made obstacles and mines. The boat plowed forward to water that was only about ankle high which allowed the men to hit the beach running. They were not bogged down as they waded through chest-high water (or deeper) and exposed to machine gun fire that would kill them before hitting the sand. He followed the men in front of him as he began his sprint to the beach. He heard rounds of machine gun fire whizzing past his head, some hitting the water all around him as he quickly moved onto the sand. Several more GIs right in front of him went down…but he pressed on running for his life. Artillery shells exploding everywhere around him!

"How would it feel when I get hit? I hope it's quick…right in the head if I'm going to get it!" He thought as many more of his fellow soldiers were blown apart.

His commanders told him earlier that there would be large holes blown in the sand from the Allied bombers that were supposed to have dropped thousands of tons of bombs several hours before the invasion to provide natural cover for the GIs when they hit the beach. There were no such holes. The bombers were delayed out of England because of bad weather and the Army Air Force Pilots were afraid there was a possibility of hitting the allied troops already on the beach. They dropped their payloads inland that left thousands of dead livestock and some very confused French farmers… but the beaches remained pristine.

Busi looked for the holes as he got closer to the sand but saw nothing but heads, arms, legs and dead bodies strewn over seventy-five yards of flat open sand, obviously the result of the doomed first wave. German pillboxes tucked in the sides of the bluffs above the beach were zeroed in on the Higgins Boats as they came ashore. As they raked the shoreline with machine gun fire the only GIs that would survive were the lucky ones. There were so many landing crafts and so many GIs that the Germans literally could not shoot all of them as they moved their machine guns up and down the shoreline.

As Busi continued to run onto the beach, a blizzard of machine gun fire screamed past him. He heard an incoming artillery round whining overhead. He sensed the round was going to be close and thought this may be his end. The shell landed about twenty-five feet behind him…a direct hit on the very Higgins Boat that brought him ashore. The shell obliterated the boat and the remaining soldiers that were positioned toward the back. They never had a chance. Busi, hearing the incoming shell, dove on his belly, face first into the sand almost simultaneously with another lucky GI right next to him. As the shell hit, he looked back and saw pieces of human body parts flying everywhere along with chunks of the Higgins Boat. Smoke billowed from the wreckage and the remaining body parts washed ashore with the surf. He had no idea how many men were still on the barge when the shell hit, but the sight of the explosion was overwhelming.

"What was happening? It wasn't supposed to be this bad." He thought to himself as he tried to become invisible.

The Private frantically pushed sand up in front of his head to try to give himself a little protection from the enemy guns. Within seconds he had created a small sand barrier between his head and certain death. Rounds were hitting the sand in front of him shortly after building the barrier. He wildly dug deeper into the sand under him until there was a crude, but formidable hole that seemed to work, at least for now. He looked over at his fellow soldier two feet away and tried screaming at him through the deafening sounds of the battle.

"*God damn it, are we catching hell!*" He screamed making sure he didn't pick up his head even an inch.

"Are you alright?" Busi asked as he grabbed the man with his left arm.

As he moved the GI slightly he saw an awful sight. His fellow soldier had been shot through the head. The bullet went through his skull and penetrated his back.

"*Holy Jesus*! *God damn it*!" He screamed as more rounds ripped through the sand around him. He had never been more scared in his life.

Private Busi was so busy digging he hadn't noticed that the GI next to him never moved from the time they both hit the sand. Although Busi didn't know him, he felt sick again and realized how lucky he had been up to now, but the battle raged on. After a few minutes of not moving at all, Private Busi began to wonder who was really the lucky one. Maybe it would be better to just get it over with right now…right on this beach. After all the war was over for the poor GI next to him he thought, staring at the lifeless body two feet away.

Screams of the wounded and dying were everywhere around him. The smell of smoke and death were overpowering. As he looked out of his crude hole down the beach, the sight of hundreds of dead and dying soldiers was everywhere. If he had ever imagined what hell was like, this was it. He tried not to think about it. All he needed to do was to survive this battle and he would be fine. That mindset became his mantra and as time would prove, it served him well.

He lay paralyzed on the sand, trying not to move and risk being spotted by the enemy looking down at him just a few hundred yards up the bluff. The battle raged on and just when he thought he might be able to get up and run toward the bluffs a new wave of gunfire, mortars and artillery would rain down on him. So he lay there, for hours in the same hole, watching as more Higgins barges approached the shore and were blown to bits. He could hear the agonizing screams of the wounded that lay helpless on the beach. There would be no medics to treat their wounds. Any medic that tried to treat a wounded soldier on the open beach would himself become a casualty.

He observed the German Artillery score direct hits on the Allied ships well offshore. Hundreds more GIs scrambled off their barges only to be cut down by a hale of machine gun fire from the bluffs above Omaha. Only a few survived. It was a grizzly sight. Dog Red was a mess and in total chaos. He continued to lie in his makeshift hole, pinned down by enemy fire. It was as if the Germans had a machine gun zeroed in on his position.

The Jeeps and trucks that were supposed to follow his unit had not come ashore as yet. So he waited and watched. The few survivors of his squad were scattered everywhere. Some had dug in on the beach… some made it to the seawall, but for the most part they were disorganized and not going anywhere. The German guns had complete control of Dog Red, at least for now, as they continued to slaughter American GIs as they landed.

Busi's orders were simple. Hit the beach at Dog Red, eliminate any enemy strongholds and wait for the Jeeps and trucks to arrive. He and his men were to then proceed up the Les Moulins Draw (one of four draws to be taken that day) to the top of the bluffs. There, he was to wait until June 7th when the rest of the Second Infantry Division would land at Omaha Beach and meet at the top of the bluffs near the small town of St. Laurent. They would then have new orders to proceed. The Germans had other plans.

He assessed the current situation. First, as far as he could tell, there were no more than four or five men in his squad of fifteen that were still alive. Second, they were all pinned down for hours now and any attempt to move closer to the bluffs would be certain death. Third, no trucks, no Jeeps, no tanks and any lucky GI that made it on to the beach was totally disorganized and disoriented just trying to stay alive. There was absolutely nothing he could do and no place to go. So he waited. He noticed, after several hours, that the landings on Omaha had ceased. The Higgins Boats were no longer coming ashore as they were earlier and that became a concern. He had no idea what was happening.

By 1300 hours (1:00 PM), five and half hours after Private Busi hit Dog Red, General Norman Cota with his Fifth Battalion Rangers managed to secure the ST. Laurent Draw. Cota landed on Easy Green (Busi's left flank) at about 0745 hours (7:45 AM). He was headed for St. Laurent and Colleville, two small French towns about a quarter of a mile inland from the beaches. With Cota's success, the German dominance began to wane at Easy Green and Easy Red.

By 1500 hours (3:00 PM) the machine gun fire began to lighten and Private Busi was able to move closer to the bluffs with a handful of men. Still with no support and little firepower he believed that the Jeeps and trucks surely would be landing soon.

What he didn't know was that General Omar Bradley, Commander of U.S. Forces on Omaha and Utah Beaches, had cancelled all further landings on Omaha. Bradley, not knowing of Cota's progress, became extremely worried that the five thousand soldiers already ashore on Omaha were all stranded and pinned down. Any further landings would crowd the beach and make it easier for the German guns to slaughter the incoming GIs. He considered ordering all remaining landings diverted to Utah Beach.

That would have sealed the fate of the men on Omaha. With no support to follow them, Busi and his men would have succumbed to complete annihilation or capture by the Germans. Bradley knew this and decided to wait.

By 1500 (3:00 P.M.) hours Bradley had received confirmation that Cota and his small group of men had overrun several German positions on the bluff and was now returning from the unoccupied town of Vierville, a quarter of a mile from the beach.

Bradley now decided against sending all additional landings to Utah and gave the orders to continue landings at Omaha. Private Busi began to move again as fire from the German pillboxes, although still extremely heavy, was beginning to subside at least enough to get out of his hole and try to organize what was left of his squad. The landings on Omaha resumed and Busi felt relieved that he had not been abandoned. He had been lying in his makeshift hole for almost six hours! As the tide moved in closer to his hole he saw the red water from the blood of the doomed first and second wave of soldiers. Any movement on his part prior to now would have been certain death. But his patience had paid off and he would live to fight another day.

As he began to move among some of the men, he realized that many of the soldiers he thought were alive were actually dead. As the tide came in, the water washing up on the shore was red from the blood of the slaughtered GIs. Body parts were everywhere along the beach. He had no idea it would be this bad. It was hard for him to believe what he was seeing, so he again tried to put it out of his mind and just survive.

His orders were clear…wait for the Jeeps and trucks. So like the good soldier he was, he waited with the few troops that were still alive. Busi and his men were now able to see the bluffs clearly and locate the positions of the German pillboxes. He still had little support and few troops so his only choice was to remain defensive and return fire at anything that moved on the bluffs above him. Still there were no vehicles and no support.

The Les Moulins Draw that he and his men were supposed to move on was the last draw to be cleared at 2000 hours (8:00

P.M.). General Cota had to backtrack from the Vierville Draw to attack the Les Moulins Draw from behind. German Infantry and numerous pillboxes heavily fortified the draw. This would explain the almost impossible task for Busi and his men to move up this draw or even to move off Dog Red. Although Cota had cleared the draw there were still many German pillboxes that remained untouched on the bluffs above Dog Red. These German positions continued to wreak havoc on Busi and his men still pinned down on the beach.

As darkness began to fall over what became known as "Bloody Omaha," Private Busi remained on the beach. The German blizzard of bullets had begun to subside. Although many of the German positions above Dog Red were still viable, visibility as well as the daylight was rapidly waning.

The remaining German positions along the beach were also running out of ammunition, reinforcements and other supplies. The Allied Paratroopers dropped behind the German lines on the night of June 5th, along with the advancing units from the beaches, were cutting off all possible escape routes and the German supply lines to the rear. The German positions at Dog Red were the last to be cleared that evening from the rear.

The Private with just a handful of men began to move around the beach, firing sporadically at the targets above as darkness fell. It became eerily quiet. Occasional German artillery rounds could be heard overhead screaming toward the armada of ships in the Channel. Intermittent bursts of machine gun fire could be heard up the draw and on the bluff. Busi remained on the beach. The Jeeps and trucks never arrived and any attempt to go up the draw with the small contingent of soldiers was extremely risky at night.

He decided it would be best to dig in for the night and stay put. The rest of the Second Division would be landing in the morning and he would wait for support and new orders at that time. It was a cold and drizzly night on the beach, but he and his men, who had survived the worst of D-Day, remained there all night.

As Busi lay in his foxhole that night he began to shake. Was it the damp, cold air and light drizzle of the miserable North Sea night or the realization of what had just transpired over the previous sixteen hours? It surely was a little of both.

Sleep was impossible as the day's horrific events ran through his mind like an old movie. It seemed surreal. The death and destruction that surrounded him was beyond description.

"How did I survive? How was it possible that a guy just two feet away was killed and I survived?" he kept thinking over and over again

It was hard for him to comprehend. He contemplated, not only his survival, but also what was to come. How long would this war continue? How long would his luck hold out? If today was any indication of what was to come his chances of survival seemed slim.

Busi thought of his family, especially his mother who had worried about him since his induction. There was a good chance he would never see her again and that realization was sobering.

As the cold, miserable night dragged on he had plenty of time to think. His mind drifted back to what he thought was a terrible existence in the hills of Western Pennsylvania as a child. He chuckled to himself as he thought about the two-room shack where he grew up and the hordes of siblings running around their subsistence farm.

As the sounds of small arms fire and the occasional overhead artillery shell continued, he crouched in his sandy hole and got as comfortable as he could.

His mind was again at ease as he drifted deeper into thoughts of home and the day's events faded.

His father had given him instructions on a very important chore he expected Joe to tend to while he left for an important meeting at the coalmine where he worked. After all Joe was ten years old now and he could be trusted with such an important task.

The still that his father Andrea' had built was brewing a new batch of moonshine and it would begin producing the valuable hundred proof alcohol while he was away at the mine. He needed someone to watch the brew and make sure as the one-gallon jug began to fill up it was removed and replaced with an empty one under the spigot. If this were not done the valuable moonshine would overflow the gallon jug onto the dirt floor and be wasted.

The brew had to be in gallon jugs so that when the buyer came to pick up the illegal booze in the middle of the night the jugs could be hidden in a small hole in the ground. The jugs were also easier for the buyer to carry away from the remote location and back to town.

Andrea' was a strict disciplinarian. He expected his children to do as they were told or suffer severe consequences and corporal punishment. He did not spare the rod. He knew that if he told his son Joe to do a chore, it would be done correctly or Joe would suffer the consequences.

As Andrea' left his son to his chore he walked up the hill and out of sight. Joe ran though the snow into the family's three-room shack and grabbed his brothers Pete and Frank. Frank was eight and Pete was six.

"Let's go! Papa gave me an important job to do and I want you two to help me!" He said in a high-pitched, excited voice.

"What is it Joe?" Pete asked.

"I have to watch the still! Come on!" Joe replied as he turned toward the door.

"Oh boy! Let's go! This is gonna' to be fun!" the two younger brothers shouted as they ran out the front door with Joe.

The three made there way toward the still through the cold January air with three feet of snow covering the ground. The still was only a few hundred feet from the house but was completely invisible to anyone who might wander on to the premises.

In 1930 prohibition was in full swing and anyone caught making, drinking or for that matter, possessing alcohol would feel the full brunt of the federal government. Andrea', a shrewd Italian Immigrant had devised an ingenious way to manufacture the product out of sight of even the most suspicious Federal Agent. The hills of Western Pennsylvania provided perfect cover for the illegal operation. On the side of his two room shanty a hill rose up to the main dirt road.

Andrea' dug into the side of the hill deep enough to carve out a small eight foot square room with a small slanted door on the side of the hill for access. The door was covered with dirt and weeds in the summer and snow in the winter leaving a totally hidden room in the side of the hill. There was room for his still, a small bar made from barrels and some ply wood and an area for the storage of many gallons of the illegal substance. It was perfect.

He had some connections with a few of the town's people to purchase the moonshine from him. Andrea' would pass the word that the moonshine was brewed and the buyer would come out to the remote farm at two or three in morning. The buyer would take several gallons of the moonshine from the designated hole and leave usually a few dollars per gallon in an envelope in the same hole. Andrea' would go to the hole the next morning and retrieve his booty. It was as illegal as hell, but it sure helped Andrea' feed twelve hungry mouths around the farm.

The three young boys reached the door and looked around to make sure no one was watching. They quickly brushed the cold snow away from side of the hill exposing the small wooden door that opened into the room with thee still. They quickly opened the door, jumped inside and closed the door behind them. It was totally dark. Joe struck a match he had in his hand and the room quickly lit up. He walked over to the lantern hanging over the makeshift bar that consisted of a few wooden planks propped up on two barrels at each end of the planks. He lit the lantern and the whole room lit up.

He could see that the first jug was already half full as the clear liquid continued to drain into the gallon jug.

"Wow. Look at it. It's really goin' now. Joe said as the three boys gathered around the still.

"Yea, look at it!" Pete confirmed.

"Hey, let's play bar tender. Pete you be the bar tender and Joe and me will be your customers, just like Papa does down in Edri!" Frank said.

"Yea, that'll be fun Joe. Come on!" Pete jumped in.

"OK, let's do it!" Joe replied.

He went over to the half full jug and removed it from under the spigot. He placed an empty jug back under the spigot and brought the half full jug over to the bar. Pete walked around behind the planks and was hardly tall enough to reach the bar. He stood on an old stool and leaned over the planks.

"What'll you have boys?" Pete asked Joe and Frank.

"We'll have a whiskey bar tender!" Joe replied as he and Frank bellied up to the opposite side of the bar.

Pete reached to the corner of the bar where Andrea' always kept several shot glasses for sampling the moonshine.

He grabbed two glasses and plunked them in front of Joe and Frank. He could hardly lift the half full gallon jug so Frank had to help him pour the moonshine in the two glasses. When the glasses were full Joe and Frank slugged the full shot glasses down their throats just like they had seen their father do hundreds of times before. Both boys' faces turned red and the two started coughing. The one hundred percent alcohol burned like fire all the way down their throats. They continued to cough as they tried to get control of themselves.

"Man, that was terrible!" Frank could hardly whisper the words.

"Yea, that's bad but if you drink more it gets better!" Joe said through his coughing spell.

The two boys bellied up to the bar again.

"I'll have another bar tender!" Joe demanded.

"Me too!" Frank joined in.

Pete took the jug and poured two more drinks for his customers. Joe and Frank looked at each other as they picked up their glasses again. Joe slugged his full glass and Frank followed. The two again started coughing and began laughing as they walked around trying to calm the burning sensation in their throats.

Pete watched in amazement from behind the bar as the two came back to the bar and told him to set up another round.

After three more rounds of this insanity the two began to get sick.

"I don't feel very good Joe." Frank looked at Joe.

"Me either. I think I'm gonna' to puke." Joe replied.

The two staggered over the door and fumbled with the latch to get it open. It was almost impossible for either of them to remain standing. Pete came out from behind the bar and ran over to help open the door. As Pete opened the door the two boozers stumbled outside into the frozen air, got about three feet from the door and stopped. Both boys put their hands on their knees, bent over and puked out all the contents of their stomachs. Pete watched in shock as the two continued their projectile vomiting.

Joe took one more step and fell face first into the snow completely unconscious. Frank never took a step. He fell forward into the snow that had soaked up his vomit also unconscious. Pete ran to the house as fast as he could to get Mario, Joe's oldest brother by three years.

Pete ran to the second bedroom where Mario was helping clean the large room that housed all ten children

"Mario, come quick. Joe and Pete are passed out in the snow!" Pete screamed at his brother.

Mario dropped the broom he was holding and ran out with Pete.

"What happened?" Mario asked Pete.

"I don't know. We were playing bar tender and Joe and Frank got sick." Pete replied as the two made their way to the door.

They both ran outside to where the two boozers were slumped unconscious in the snow.

"Oh God! What the hell were you guys doin'?" Mario asked as he knelt down beside Frank.

"Forget it. Help me get him up!" Mario continued.

Mario and Pete picked up Frank, still unconscious. Mario grabbed him with both arms and carried him into the house.

"Mama!" Mario yelled.

Josephine, their mother appeared and was shocked to see Mario with Frank in his arms and Pete running behind.

"What happened?" she shouted.

"Aw, Frank and Joe got in Papa's still and they drank too much moonshine." Mario answered.

"Put them both on our bed." She instructed Mario.

Mario carried Frank into the parents' bedroom and laid him on the bed. He ran back outside and picked up Joe. He laid Joe next to Frank on the bed and the two slept for hours. Josephine looked in on the two as they slept off their drunk concerned that they had drank too much of the pure alcohol.

Joe woke up first and looked around his mother's darkened room. His head felt like someone hit him with a hammer. Frank came back to life shortly after Joe and the two contemplated what had happened.

"God, do I feel sick…my head." Joe couldn't even finish his sentence.

"Papa's gonna' kill us!" Frank replied.

"Why are we in Papa's bed?" Joe asked.

No one ever stepped foot into Andrea's room let alone slept in his bed.

"I don't know but we're gonna' catch a whoopin'." Frank replied.

"I don't care, I just want to die." Joe responded through his pain.

The two lay in the parents' bed for several more hours and finally were able to stand and walk.

Andrea' had returned home two hours after the incident and heard what happened. He looked in on the sleeping boys to make sure they weren't too ill. He knew that if they had drank any more than they did, they could have easily died. Andrea' said nothing to the boys about the incident as they began to regain their health. It would be two more days before Joe and Frank felt "normal" again. Andrea' realized that the pain and suffering they experienced from their mistake was punishment enough.

There would be no further punishment handed out by Andrea' or Josephine and Joe's parents never spoke of the incident again.

Frank and Joe learned a valuable lesson that day and they would never again take another sip of their father's moonshine.

A German artillery shell whistled over the Private's head and exploded just off shore as he snapped back to the reality of the war. He popped his head out of his hole and looked around the darkness of Bloody Omaha. He thought to himself that this wasn't Pennsylvania and he had a lot more to worry about than his father's discipline.

*NOTE: Five beaches made up the assault on occupied France on June 6th 1944. Three beaches, Gold, Juno and Sword were taken by

British and Canadian troops. The U.S First Army assaulted the other two, Omaha and Utah. Of the five beaches, Omaha was by far the bloodiest, deadliest and most heavily defended. Fifty seven thousand, five hundred American Troops landed on Omaha and Utah Beaches. The first Allied battle of the European Theater left over three thousand, five hundred American dead and wounded and the war against the Nazis was not even twenty-four hours old. The battle hardened 352nd German Infantry Division was dug in at Omaha and this very tough fighting unit caused most of the casualties on June 6th. *(Source - *D-Day 24 Hours That Saved the World – Time*)

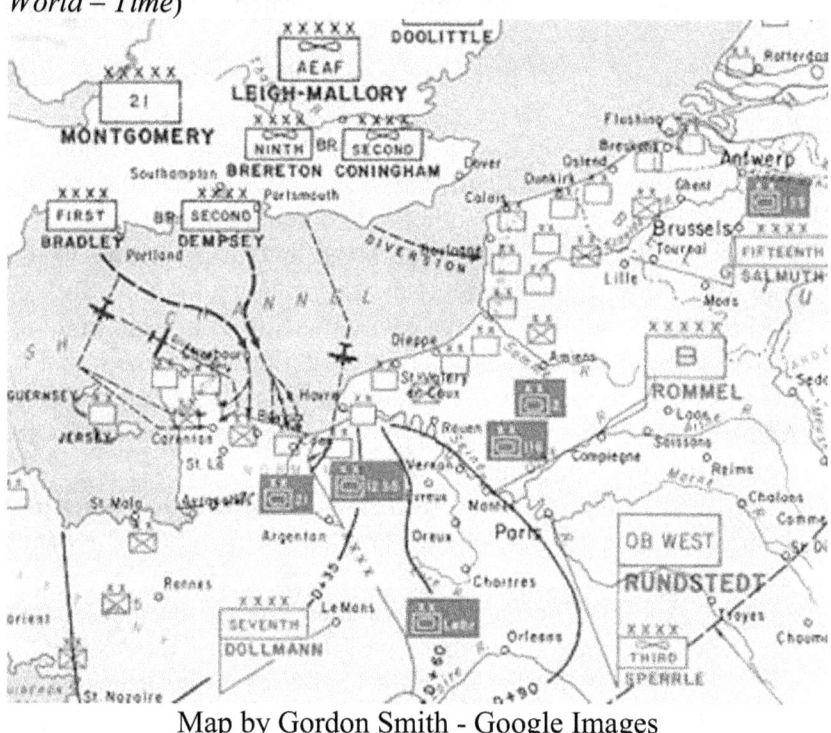

Map by Gordon Smith - Google Images

Then Buck Private Busi – Second Row – Fifth from Left. Company D (partial) – Ninth Infantry Regiment - 2nd I.D. Camp McCoy, Wisconsin 1942
Photo courtesy of Sergeant Joseph Busi

Indianhead Patch
Insignia of the Second Infantry Division
Photo by Google Images

Chapter 2
No Day of Rest
June 7th : D-Day Plus One

As dawn approached on D-Day plus one, Private Busi emerged from his foxhole on Dog Red to witness a sight that gave him hope and eased some of the tension in his gut. The Second Infantry Division began to push ashore on Omaha Beach.

Enemy defenses had been rendered impotent, as the four draws had been mostly cleared throughout June 6th. Although the German artillery still persisted with sporadic salvos toward the Armada offshore, the beaches and the bluffs above Omaha were relatively safe. The Allies were able to secure a fingernail hold on that narrow strip of beach, and several hundred yards into the French countryside. The Allied Paratroopers that had been dropped behind the German lines on June 5th hampered German reinforcements. Whatever was left of the primary German troops in Normandy pulled back to the south to regroup, leaving many snipers, mines and sporadic pockets of resistance. The Allied invasion of June 6th was a success, although, to the individual it appeared the operation was one of utter chaos and total confusion.

Private Busi took time to look back on the narrow stretch of beach that was the horror of Bloody Omaha. As the tens of thousands of soldiers of the Second Division struggled ashore past the horrific array of twisted steel, half sunken hulks of Higgins boats and the thousands of mangled, decimated bodies of the dead GIs, he knew that none of these new arrivals could ever have imagined what it was like. Except for the heroic soldiers who experienced June 6th first hand, no one could ever possibly imagine the death and hideous sights he had seen that day. Busi realized, as he watched the troops come ashore, that the only reason he was still alive was nothing more than pure luck. He also knew that what lay ahead was a day-to-day struggle for survival, and he hoped his luck would hold out.

He reported to his commanding officer, Captain Hancock who was concerned that none of the fifteen "special duty" rangers had survived the blood bath at Omaha.

"Private Busi reporting sir." Busi blurted out as he approached Hancock.

The captain looked surprised to see him. Hancock knew Private Busi and the other fourteen "special duty" rangers since he had hand picked the fifteen men during training in Northern Ireland to carry out the dangerous task of preparing the vehicles that came ashore.

"Pretty rough yesterday hey Private?" Hancock snapped.

"Yes sir, very tough resistance." Busi replied.

"What's your report soldier?"

"Sir, after we hit the beach our boat was hit by an eighty-eight. I don't know how many men made it to shore. Enemy fire was relentless, and all we could do was dig in. Movement was impossible and I waited for hours for the Jeeps and trucks to come ashore, but they never came. I tried to find the rest of my squad, but most of them are dead. If any of them survived, they're scattered somewhere along this beach. It was pretty chaotic, sir." Busi tried not to let his emotions get in the way of his report.

"Most of the Jeeps and trucks never made it to shore on the first or second wave. They'll be unloading those vehicles in the next few hours…no need for you to stay here. The engineers will remove the engine covers. Good job staying alive, private." Hancock said with a bit of pride in his voice.

"Thank you Sir."

"I'll find what's left of your squad and reassign some replacements. Report to the assembly area on this beach with Sergeant Babin. You'll receive your orders there. None of those areas up the bluffs are totally cleared. We have reports of snipers and small pockets of resistance so stay alert and pass the word." Hancock had a look of concern.

"Yes Sir." Busi responded.

Private Busi was reunited with the Ninth Infantry as the Second Division continued to come ashore. Only three of the fifteen special duty Rangers had survived D-Day and Busi was one of them.

Busi's First Sergeant Babin was also surprised to see him and there was an instant air of respect for him by his First Sergeant. The very fact that he had survived the death and destruction of June 6th told Babin that Private Busi had accomplished something that many other soldiers could not. Throughout the coming months, Sgt. Babin and Captain Hancock would find out that this soldier was not the ordinary GI, and the respect they gave him that day was well deserved.

As the Ninth Regiment began to get organized, Private Busi was glad to see his buddies from the Second Squad arrive. As they joined him one by one they congratulated him for making the landing in one piece. Their crude jokes and smiles made the horror of the previous day more bearable, but still unforgettable. Together since basic training at Camp McCoy Wisconsin, nearly two years earlier, a sense of camaraderie and brotherhood tied these men together. Their very survival depended on each man protecting one another in the face of a brutal enemy and incomprehensible conditions. The eight men who would become Busi's closest friends and brothers-in-arms were together again.

Private John "Peepsite" Amon was a quiet man they called "Peepsite" because his eyes were small like BBs. He would become the closest to Busi as time went by.

Private First Class Steven Wells was a squad leader and Busi's #2 gunner.

Private Robert Sultzaberger was another close friend.

Private "Red" Clayton was a large man they called "Red" because he had thick, red hair and freckles.

Private Dock Snyder
Private John Harrigan
Private Eldon Davis
Private Ed Rothenberry

As the morning hours passed, Busi's thoughts drifted back to the previous day and the horrors he witnessed. He looked at his buddies as they milled around and wondered how many of them would survive. After what he had seen he knew that none of them had any idea of what it was like or what was to come.

Many new replacements were ordered to fill the slots of the dead GIs that landed on the beaches that day and this would be a recurring problem Busi would face throughout the coming months. As more GIs in Busi's squad were killed, more "green" replacements were sent to fill their spots. Private Busi learned early on not to get too personal with these men because he knew they probably would not be around very long.

First Sergeant Babin reorganized Busi's Section (sixteen men) into two squads of eight. Tech Sergeant Hughes was in charge of Busi (Second squad) and the First Squad making up the First Section. Tech Sergeant Briley was in charge of the Second Section and together the two Sections formed a platoon of thirty-two men. Busi was not fond of either Hughes or Briley. Their nasty and condescending attitudes toward their underlings were not appreciated by any of the men in the platoon. Their rough and tough exteriors would later be tested in battle and prove to be a facade.

Even Capt. Hancock, their commanding officer, had a dislike for both men, but their battle worthiness had yet to be tested. Hancock would hold his final judgment of both leaders until they were tested in the heat of battle.

The reorganization took place on Omaha and their orders were to climb the St. Moulins Bluff and meet at the staging area just outside the town of St. Laurent-sur-Mer, where the Second Division Headquarters would be established.

As Busi and his squad moved up the bluff toward St. Laurent- sur- Mer they passed many German bunkers strewn with dead American and German bodies. The debris of war was everywhere. Snipers and localized pockets of German resistance hampered their movement to the staging area.

A house not far from the top of St. Moulins Draw was a particular problem as P.F.C. Busi and his squad approached. A sniper tucked away on the second floor had taken several shots from a bedroom window, at the approaching GIs. Unsure of how many of the enemy was inside, the squad approached the house cautiously from the left and right flanks. Several men approached straight up the front to draw fire from the sniper. More shots were fired at the three GIs approaching from the front. One flank closed in and entered the house abruptly through one of the side entrances blown away by some previous shelling. Busi, Hughes and two others climbed the stairs to the second floor to confront the sniper. As they approached the closed door to one of the upstairs bedrooms they could hear more shots firing from inside the room.

They had their sniper. At once two men smashed the door off it's hinges and as the door fell to the floor the four GIs swung their M1s into the room and opened up a non- stop barrage of fire on the unsuspecting sniper. Bullets blasted through every part of the room including the sniper kneeling at the window. As the startled sniper turned towards the men in surprise, rounds from the M1s tore apart the body. The sniper was not the only one surprised this morning. As the GIs stopped firing and approached the lifeless body what they saw was all to clear. The sniper was not a German soldier, but a French woman sympathetic to the Nazis. It seems the Nazis convinced this young French women that the Allies were the enemy. As the Nazis retreated the French sympathizer stayed behind to give the Allies some resistance. Unfortunately for the woman sympathizer, it meant death.

No one said a word. The squad made sure the body was lifeless, removed her rifle and left the house. There would be many more similar incidents in the coming months and for the infantry soldier, snipers (Nazi sympathizers as well as the Nazi's themselves) would become one of the most feared aspects of the war.

As the Ninth Infantry and the rest of the Second Division assembled in an area outside the town of St. Laurent-sur-Mer, Busi and the rest of his squad began to prepare for what would be nine weeks of hell in the hedgerows of Northern France.

Chapter 3
Hedgerow Hell and the Silver Star
June 9th – July 10th

Private Busi was trained as a number one gunner. He was one of a two-man team trained on the setup and use of the thirty-caliber M1917A1 water-cooled machine gun. This was an ominous weapon that fired four to six hundred rounds per minute and had a range of over one thousand yards. It was classified as a "heavy machine gun," and heavy it was...it weighed over ninety pounds with its tripod and water! The #1 gunner usually carried the gun itself, while the #2 gunner carried the tripod, water and ammo. Busi's machine gun along with his #2 gunner, Private Wells, arrived on June 7th and the two soldiers prepared themselves.

From June 9th and the attack on the town of Trevierres to the first week of July and the Second Division's approach to St. Lo, Busi's squad fought bravely with many casualties as the hedge row fighting continued. The Division was successful in pushing back elements of the famed German 352nd and the 716th Infantry. P.F.C. Busi's concerns about Wells had long disappeared as the two GIs fought side by side for weeks.

The hedgerows of Northern France were one of the worst obstacles the Allies faced during the early months of fighting. A hedgerow is a large mound of dirt, usually about four to six feet high with a row of hedges running along the very top of the mound. These hedgerows were man-made and formed hundreds of years earlier to act as natural fences in the Normandy Region of France by farmers to keep their livestock from roaming all over the French countryside.

They usually had a small opening somewhere along the mound with metal bars across so farmers could allow their livestock to move between these rows. For the allies, they were extremely dangerous. There were thousands of them and in order for the Allies to advance, soldiers and tanks would have to climb over the top and advance into the open field between the mounds to the next hedgerow. Unfortunately, hidden behind the next hedgerow was the enemy with untold numbers of soldiers and weapons waiting to slaughter the advancing GIs.

On the morning of July 9th Private Busi's section along with Sgt. Briley's section began an advance over yet another hedgerow. As they approached the top the Germans situated about one hundred yards behind the next hedgerow began throwing everything they had at the two American squads trying to advance. Mortars, machine gun fire and German made burp guns opened fire on the battle weary GIs. Along with Busi's platoon was a Sherman tank assigned to advance with the men. As Busi and Wells set up their machine gun on the top of the hedgerow to return fire, the Sherman tank began up the back side of the mound and reached the crest of the hedgerow.

Busi and Wells watched as the tank approached. As the tank began to reach the crest of the hedgerow the underside of the Sherman was exposed for just a few seconds as it slowly crept over the mound. At that split second the Germans fired an eighty-eight millimeter artillery round at the Sherman, striking it directly in it's most vulnerable area…it's underbelly.

The Sherman burst into flames as the front end collapsed on to the top of the hedgerow.

Busi and Wells watched in horror as the tank began to explode in flames. But what they saw next infuriated them even more. The two GIs in the tank were still alive and as they tried several times to open the turret hatch to get out of the burning tank, the Germans sprayed the turret with machine gun fire. They had a gun fixed on the turret and any attempt by the two men inside to escape the burning tank would be certain death. They could either be shot trying to escape or burn to death in the flaming inferno. Busi became enraged. He could hardly watch as the GIs made several more attempts to escape the burning tank only to be fired upon and forced back into their burning death trap.

"We've got to do something!" Busi screamed at Wells.

Wells just stared at Busi. He could see the Private was seething at the sight of the GIs pinned down in the burning Sherman, but he knew there was nothing they could do…at least nothing he could think of other than something foolish that could get them all killed.

"Nazi bastards! I'll fix those sons of bitches!" Busi screamed again at Wells.

Wells got nervous as Busi reached for the thirty-caliber machine gun.

"What the hell are you doing Joe?" Wells screamed back at the half crazed Private.

"Take the ammo out of the box." Busi yelled.

"What the he…"

"Just do it now God damn it."

Wells didn't wait another second. He grabbed the box of thirty caliber shells and immediately dumped out over 500-strapped rounds of ammo on the ground.

Busi grabbed one end of the banded shells and loaded the Heavy. He lifted the forty-pound machine gun off the tripod. He grabbed the asbestos glove that every machine gun team was issued (this glove protected the gunner from the extreme heat of the gun barrel when it came time to move the gun after firing for a long period of time).

He donned the glove on his left hand and with the monster machine gun cradled in his arms, five hundred rounds of ammo trailing behind him, stood up over the top of the hedgerow. He began walking down the front side of the mound firing wildly with the thirty-caliber against his right hip in the direction of the next hedgerow one hundred yards away. He swung the monster in his arms back and forth to make sure he sprayed as many bullets in all directions as he could. Wells was dumbfounded.

"Busi, get back here. You're gonna' get yourself killed." He shouted in vane at the crazed Private.

Busi was not about to listen. He continued to fire wildly and advance slowly. As the monster gun fired, the recoil action kept holding him back as he tried to advance more quickly. He knew the longer he continued to fire the better chance the GIs in the tank would have to escape their burning inferno. He also knew that the longer he was exposed to the enemy the better chance he had of being killed. It didn't matter to him now. He was too far along to go back as he made his way through the open field. It was working. As soon as he began firing, the Germans ducked for cover and stopped firing at the tank. They became confused as the crazed Private began firing. Not knowing where the firing was coming from, the Germans decided to keep their heads down. It was long enough for the tankers to open their turret hatch and escape the burning Sherman.

They jumped out of the tank and headed down the backside of the hedgerow to safety. Private Busi's life hung in the balance as he slowly made his way through the open field still firing what was left of the five-hundred rounds dragging beside him. The monster machine gun began to smoke in his hands as the water-cooled barrel began to heat up. He continued traversing his fire, moving slowly, as the recoil hampered his forward motion.

Sergeant Hughes, Briley and the thirty plus men in their squads perched on top of the hedgerow, watched in amazement as Private Busi slowly made his way across the thigh high weeds of the open field totally unscathed…but his luck was about to run out…at least somewhat!

A German rifleman positioned on Busi's left flank spotted him and squeezed off a round at the crazed GI, just before Busi's gun came around again to his position. The German bullet struck the ammo belt about a foot from the ground and creased one of the thirty caliber rounds in the ammo belt. As Busi looked down he could see the damaged ammo belt and knew all too well what was about to happen.

As the damaged thirty-caliber shell approached and entered the gun it jammed the firing pin and the gun stopped firing. Private Busi was now almost dead center in the middle of the open field with a jammed machine gun and no more ammo. He threw the heavy down in front of him and dove on his belly with only the three-foot high weeds for cover. He quickly covered his head with his arms expecting to be blown to bits any second by a Nazi eighty-eight millimeter artillery round. The Germans were experts with the eighty-eight and he knew it. He knew they could blow his ass to chop meat if they had only a slight inkling of his position. He waited, for what seemed like an eternity, for the inevitable. It never came. There was an eerie quiet that seemed to give him hope.

"Ammo! Ammo!" Busi screamed as loud as he could.

Wells heard his cry for more ammo and quickly gathered another box of thirty caliber shells, but realized he would now have to make his way in the open field to give Busi the ammo.

"Get that man some more ammo. Sgt. Briley screamed.

Wells had no choice. He crawled down the side of the hedgerow on his belly dragging a box of thirty-caliber ammo with him. The weeds provided good cover since they were so high. Wells crawled on his belly until he got within twenty feet of Busi. Wells took the box of ammo and threw it as far as he could toward Busi. It landed right behind him. Busi reached back, grabbed the box and began dumping out the cartridges staying as close to the ground as he could.

"Joe, you're gonna' get us both killed you crazy bastard." Wells blurted out.

"Sorry Wells, but I'm gonna' kill every one of those bastards. You just stay down." Joe replied.

"Are you nuts? There's probably a whole platoon back there with an eighty-eight to boot." Wells shouted back.

"There won't be when I'm done." Busi replied as if he were possessed.

"Just stay down."

Private Busi stood up, picked up the Heavy and began again where he had left off. He fired wildly, traversing back and forth into the far hedgerow and to the flanks in case any of the enemy had advanced on his sides. Not one German gun had returned fire. Busi made his way through the rest of the open field to the very edge of the enemy hedgerow, right behind a huge oak tree, just on his side of the hedge. He dropped the heavy on the ground and slammed himself against the side of the hedgerow and the huge tree. He was totally out of breath, and tried desperately to gain his composure.

The enemy, as far as he knew, was just on the other side of the hedgerow. He could hear the Germans screaming as if in chaos and not very far away. He climbed to the top of the hedgerow and peaked over the top. He was amazed at what he saw. The last five or six German soldiers were climbing over the next hedgerow seventy-five yards away yelling as if a ghost was chasing them. An entire German platoon had retreated to the next hedgerow for fear of being over run.

Private Busi began laughing aloud as if he were completely crazy. He continued laughing almost uncontrollably. Tears began to run down his face he laughed so hard. Was it his sanity that had begun to crack or just the thought of what he had just done that made him lose control. It didn't matter and he didn't think about it. He quickly ran down the side of the hedgerow and picked up the thirty caliber and what was left of the cartridges. He stumbled back up to the top of the hedgerow and threw the Heavy down on the soft dirt. The four-inch metal rod attached to the bottom of the weapon stuck in the ground that now allowed him stability to fire and traverse the gun.

"Come out and fight you fucking Nazi bastards...Come out and fight. Come on...come on." He was now shouting at the top of his lungs.

A German rifleman, as if responding to Busi's offer appeared, climbed over the hedgerow, and with his rifle aiming right at the Private started walking in the open field.

"Are you kidding? *Are you kidding me?"* Busi yelled in his direction.

For the first time today, Busi aimed right down the sight of the big gun and caught the German in his cross hairs. He squeezed the trigger for a second and a burst of thirty-caliber bullets ripped into the Nazi as he fell lifeless to the ground.

"Stupid ass. Must have had too much Cognac." he mumbled to himself.

The Private had now come back to his senses and he knew that he couldn't stay in that position for long by himself so he motioned for the rest of his and Briley's squad to make their way to him.

"Let's go. Come on. Come on. He yelled as he motioned with his left arm.

Unsure if the way had been completely cleared, Briley, Hughes and the rest of the thirty-two-man section made their way toward Busi slowly, concerned about their flanks and possible German snipers. Their progress was slow as they spread out and began making their way through the weeds toward the screaming Private.

As Private Busi lay on the top of the hedgerow with his thirty caliber perched in front of him, he heard machine gun fire coming from the enemy hedgerow. Some rounds came close as he saw dirt fly up in front of him. He watched intently as more rounds went off.

"Where the hell is that coming from?" he questioned himself.

A few more enemy machine gun blasts went off.

As he watched, he saw minute puffs of smoke coming from a small opening about three feet wide in the enemy hedgerow slightly to his right (German weapons and ammunition were so well engineered that they gave off very little smoke when fired).

"I got 'em now." He shouted aloud.

He aimed the Heavy's crosshairs in the center of the opening in the enemy's hedgerow and squeezed the trigger. A hale of thirty caliber rounds ripped through the opening. Busi could see his tracers screaming through the opening as if he were tossing them in from two feet away (a tracer is every fifth bullet that lights up to give the gunner an idea of where his bullets were going). He saw utter chaos on the other side of the opening. German Soldiers were running back and forth across the opening falling, as they were being torn apart by the barrage of machine gun fire. He continued to fire.

The Heavy began to heat up as he relentlessly blasted away non-stop. The Germans had no idea what was happening. All they knew was that something or someone had a bead on their position and was wreaking havoc.

Briley and his men suddenly stopped and hit the deck. They all dove to the ground and took cover in the weeds as Busi opened fire again. Sergeant Briley looked up and saw Busi firing at the enemy and realized that the crazed Private was not done yet. Briley motioned to his men to continue forward as they watched the hero on the next hedgerow annihilate the enemy.

Busi continued to blast away for almost a full minute. The gun finally went silent. He had used the last of the ammo and the only sound he could hear was the steaming barrel of the thirty caliber that was now overheated.

The Private ducked down below the top of the hedgerow, pulled the thirty caliber down with him and rolled over on his back so his position would be unknown to any enemy soldiers who may be observing. Busi could now see the two American sections approaching through the weeds of the open field behind him. A rifleman from Briley's squad reached Busi first. He skirted up the side of the hedgerow and knelt down next to Busi. He stared at the Private as if he were and alien from another planet.

"You better get your head dow—" Busi warned the rifleman.

"Brrrrrrrrrrrrrrrp...Brrrrrrrrrrp!" Two quick bursts from a German burp gun hit the rifleman in the head right below his hairline ripping the top of his head clean off. The careless GI's helmet flew off and rolled down the back of the hedgerow. Joe couldn't even finish his sentence. The rifleman fell backwards on the back of his legs still in the kneeling position. He never knew what hit him!

"*Son of a bitch.*" Busi yelled.

Busi rushed to turn him over on his back, to see if there was a chance of saving the soldier, but realized he was dead before he fell. The top half of his head was gone. He took the dead GI's raincoat from his pack and covered him with it. Busi paused for a moment and even though he didn't know the soldier, he felt terrible. He had seen hundreds of men die in just a few weeks he had been in combat and he always felt bad.

All shooting had stopped and there was that eerie silence. Sergeants Briley and Hughes arrived at Busi's position moments later and were vigilant in keeping their heads down below the top of the hedgerow.

"I can't believe what I just saw, soldier!" Briley said starring at the Private. Busi looked at Briley and noticed the Sergeant looked extremely scared.

A medic ran up and approached the dead soldier lying

between Busi and Briley. He began to pick up the raincoat covering the GI to see if there was anything he could do.

"Don't bother...he's gone. Busi said coldly.

"I couldn't just let those guys in the tank burn up... I had to do something." Busi said, almost apologizing.

"I don't know whether to put you in for a citation or a section eight." Briley responded half joking.

He now looked petrified and pulled his left hand over the top of his helmet as some machine gun fire came from the enemy hedgerow. Busi was still in the killing mode and stared straight ahead not really hearing what the Sergeant had just told him. Sergeant Hughes approached the two men.

"What are we going to do now Private?" Hughes asked almost cowardly.

Busi looked at Hughes and saw the Sergeant was trembling. He was so scared he was almost incoherent. Busi looked at Hughes and Briley in disgust. He thought back to Northern Ireland before the war had started and how these two supposed leaders would denigrate and verbally abuse him and the other men. They weren't so tough now that there was an enemy trying to kill them.

"As far as I know Sergeant there are still some Germans on the other side of that next hedgerow and if I were you I'd get a couple more of our machine guns along the top of this hedge and let them know we're still here.... come on Sergeant use your head...get a hold of yourself. " Busi barked out at his Sergeant as if he were in command.

Hughes was frozen and stared at the Private as if he were lost. Briley was also frozen and he lay in his defensive position as Busi finished his recommendation.

"Forget it. I'll get the gunners set up." Busi growled realizing the two leaders were too scared to move.

The return fire from the enemy had stopped for now. The GIs hoped that the Germans had pulled back to regroup but Busi and his men still set up a defensive position on the hedgerow. After thirty or forty minutes there were no signs of the enemy. A patrol was sent ahead to find the position of the Germans and they reported to Hughes and Briley that as far as they could tell the Germans had pushed back more than the next few hedgerows. Hughes and Briley were positioned next to Private Busi and the Private heard the report from the patrol.

"What should we do Sergeant?" Hughes asked Briley.
Busi jumped in.

"Sergeant, we have the Jerries on the run. They don't know what the hell hit 'em and we need to keep pushing them back…now let's get the hell out of here."

Hughes and Briley couldn't argue accept for the fact that they may not have been up to the task. After several minutes of indecision, the leaders gave the order to move forward. The Platoon prepared to advance and minutes later they were on their way. There was no resistance as they made their way to the next hedgerow. They began to move more quickly and they made their way to the top of the next hedgerow. As Private Busi quickly made his way over the top of the hedgerow he looked to his right and saw dead enemy soldiers strewn everywhere on the ground. Most of the dead were in close proximity to the opening in the hedgerow he had zeroed in with his thirty caliber. He had no idea how many were killed, and he only thought about it for a moment. The Private was too busy advancing to stop and take a body count so he continued moving forward.

The Platoon took two more hedgerows in this single advance without any resistance, almost unheard of, in the hedgerows of Northern France. As darkness approached, the Platoon dug in for the night.

Busi and Wells set up their machine gun on top of the hedgerow and began alternating two-hour shifts. As one gunner slept the other manned the gun and kept watch for enemy patrols or advancements. Wells took first watch. Busi was exhausted and laid on the side of the hedgerow just below his Second gunner. As Busi lay quietly he could faintly here sounds of battle miles away. His mind drifted back to the burning Sherman and the rifleman whose head had been blown apart.

Suddenly, without warning he heard a single shot. Almost instantaneously, Wells let out a huge grunt as if he had been hit.

Joe jumped up to see Wells sliding down the side of the hedgerow almost on top of him. He grabbed Wells and turned him over on his back. Wells had both hands covering his face. As Busi pulled his hands away he saw that Wells had been shot in the face by a single bullet right below his right eye. The bullet entered his face and exited out the back of his head. Blood gushed from under Wells' eye as he moaned in pain. Joe put his finger over the hole in Wells' face to stop the gush of blood.

"*Medic! Medic*! Busi screamed as loud as he could.

"Shit, hang on Wells, they're coming.

The medics arrived in a matter of seconds and grabbed the Second gunner. They packed the hole in his face with gauze after controlling the bleeding and wrapped his entire head. Wells had been lucky. Although the bullet entered his brain, it miraculously did not do any damage as it exited out the back of his head. He had survived but paid a heavy price. Busi watched as the medics took his number two gunner away on a stretcher. Wells' fighting days were over and Private Busi never saw Wells again. The rest of the night was quiet as Joe manned his gun without sleep or a number two gunner.

As the morning of July 10th dawned, Busi and his squad prepared to move forward again. The Private noticed a hurried Staff Sergeant Babin approaching from the rear. He hustled up the side of the hedgerow where Busi was lying and knelt down next to him.

"Private, how are you?" Babin asked.

"Fine Sergeant, good to see you…what brings you up here?

"You soldier." Babin replied.

"Me?" Busi was quite surprised.

"That's right…Briley reported what you did here yesterday and Captain Hancock has decided to promote you to Sergeant and the Captain wants you take over this squad."

Busi was stunned.

"Promotion right over Corporal to Sergeant?" Busi asked.

"That's right. As of today you are now a Buck Sergeant and the leader of Second Squad." Babin was firm.

"Do you think I can do it?" Busi asked, unsure.

"Of course you can! Look, I don't know how you survived

Omaha and after Briley told me what you did back there at that hedgerow, you can lead this squad...we need leaders like you. These guys will follow you anywhere!" Babin assured the new Sergeant.

Babin was right. The men of the Second Squad saw for themselves what a leader sometimes had to do to and they all knew that Busi had put his life on the line to save the tankers.

Busi thought to himself that he had been extremely lucky so far, and really didn't understand what the big deal was about. He was just doing what he had to do to get this damn war over and go home. If the Army wanted to promote him and make him a leader than that was fine with him.

"Ok Sergeant. I'm ready to go." He replied more confidently.

"Good. And by the way Sergeant, we've also put you in for a citation for what you did." Babin said.

Busi stared at Babin in shock.

"That's not necessary Sergeant. I just wanted to get our guys out of that tank. I couldn't stand seeing them burn up in there." Busi responded.

"That's not the way I heard it Sergeant, and besides it's not up to you anyway. The report's been filed and the citation has been requested." Babin snapped back.

"Captain Hancock and me followed you up after your battle yesterday and we counted twenty-eight dead Krauts behind that hedgerow... *Twenty-eight... That's a whole platoon.*" Babin said emphatically.

"Huh...must 'a got lucky." Busi mumbled as a smile came to his face.

"Lucky my ass... no one gets that lucky...great job soldier." Babin said proudly.

"Thanks Sergeant."

Babin got back to the business at hand.

"We've got to take hill 192 and St. Lo. There should be some pretty stiff resistance from here on out, so keep these guys moving... You'll be getting your orders directly from Captain Hancock." Babin told his new Sergeant.

Don Busi

"Yes Sergeant, we're on our way." Busi replied.

Sergeant Babin patted Busi on the shoulder as he jumped up and headed down the hedgerow and back to the Command Post.

Busi now knew that Hughes and Briley were irrelevant at this point in the war and even though they were the section leaders, Sergeant Busi would be the one the fighting men and Captain Hancock would turn to for leadership. He had proven his ability to lead other men into battle by not only saving the lives of two tankers, but also killing twenty-eight of the enemy at great peril. He had created so much chaos, that he single handedly pushed back the Germans well beyond any further engagement, at least for the moment.

Note: In February 1945, Sergeant Joseph Busi was awarded the Silver Star Citation for bravery above and beyond the call of duty for his actions on July 9th 1944.

P.F.C. Wells – 2nd Gunner. Shot through the head in hedgerow country and survived.
July 9, 1944
Photo courtesy of Sergeant Joseph Busi

***M1917A1 Browning Water -cooled Machine Gun with tripod and coolant.
Nicknamed "The Heavy" because of its weight.***
Photo from www.rt66.com/~korteng/smallarms/30calhv.htm

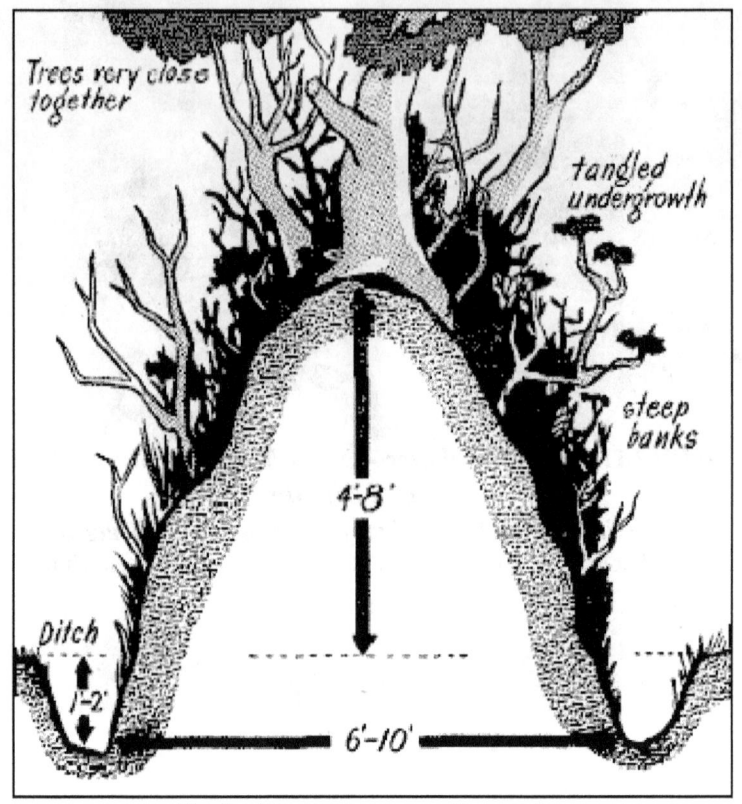

Typical hedgerow configuration
Drawing from "Lone Sentry.com" 2008

Chapter 4
Rattled Nerves
July 11th - Hill 192 - St Lo, France

Sergeants Hughes and Briley began to unravel when the war took to the hedgerows. They just couldn't cut it as leaders as time went by. Busi knew it and so did the men in both Sections. Sergeant Hughes had been losing control and was fearful of being killed or wounded. His indecisions on the field of battle were dangerous to himself and the rest of the Section. Busi, on the other hand, always seemed to have a plan even in dangerous situations. His level headedness, cool under fire and his uncanny ability to use every conceivable means to stay alive were the reasons for his survival in the war.

Hill 192 was a strategic high point just a few miles north west of the town on St. Lo, twenty-five kilometers from Omaha Beach (Hill 192 was aptly named because of it's altitude…192 meters or 624 feet above sea level). Hill 192 would be Sergeant Hughes' undoing.

The Hill was the Second Division's best-planned attack of WWII. Sergeant Busi's Second Squad, Sergeant Luther Bone's First Squad and the rest of the Ninth Infantry Regiment were to stage a diversionary attack on July 11th to detract attention from the all-out advance on Hill 192 by the 23rd and 38th Infantry Regiments to the West. After creating the diversion, the Ninth was to withdraw to its original position and go into reserve.

At 0500 hours (5:00 AM) on July 11th, the Ninth began their diversionary assault on Hill 192 after an hour of Allied artillery fire. Busi and his squad began to move up the hill and were met quickly with a German return of intense artillery fire. Sergeant Hughes and his men were positioned on a road at the bottom of the hill and were taking an incredible pounding by the German Artillery. As Busi moved up the hill he noticed that Hughes was not moving his men up the hill.

The Sergeant stopped his squad and lay flat on the side of

the hill as the artillery continued to blast the road below.

Hughes began to climb the hill alone and made his way toward Busi.

"What the hell is he doing?" Busi mumbled to himself aloud.

Hughes arrived and dove into the side of the hill next to Busi. Busi could see he was very distraught.

"Busi, where should I go with my men? You know where to be. You know these things! Where should I go?" Hughes screamed through the noise of the battle.

Busi could see he was absolutely petrified. His hands were shaking and his eyes were the size of silver dollars. He was now curled almost completely in a fetal position, hands covering his head.

Sergeant Busi tried to feel some compassion for his Sergeant but had his own crisis trying to keep himself from being blown to bits. He put down his gun and grabbed Hughes by the shirt with two hands and looked directly into his eyes.

"Sergeant Hughes. Listen to me. Get your men off that road. The Krauts are zeroed in on that road and if you stay there you're all gonna' die. Get your ass up this hill and move around to my right flank, but for God's sake get off that road. Can you understand me?" he screamed

Hughes stared back at him and shook his head.

"Yea, yea, ok." he responded.

Hughes got up and ran back down the hill. Busi could see him giving his men the signal to get off the road and up the hill. They began climbing the hill and moved to the right. Before long they disappeared from sight and Busi again gave the order to his men to continue their advance up Hill 192.

Busi would never see Sergeant Hughes again.

Sergeant Busi and the rest of the Ninth Regiment continued to divert the attention of the Germans as the 23rd and 38th Regiments began their all-out attack to the West.

The diversion worked perfectly as the Germans concentrated on the advancing Ninth Regiment. The other two Regiments made great advances West of the Ninth's position and overran the German defenses in a matter of a few hours. The German lines were pushed back to take defensive positions on the outskirts of St Lo. Its purpose accomplished, the Ninth withdrew back down Hill 192 to its original position. As Sergeant Busi withdrew back down the hill he looked for Hughes but he was gone. Busi surmised that he was either killed by the barrage or retreated before the mission was complete.

Sergeant Hughes did survive Hill 192, but was reassigned after the battle. Sergeant Busi found out after the war that Sergeant Richard Hughes was killed in action at the battle of Brest on August 30, 1944. Although Busi felt bad for Hughes it was no surprise.

Sergeant Busi knew early on in the war that every man in battle was afraid of dying, including him. From that first day on Omaha Beach he accepted the fact that he would probably be killed. He knew it and didn't try to fight it. Dwelling on his death was a pointless distraction. He carried out his orders battle after battle and was resolved to the fact that his death could come at any moment. He tried to do whatever he could to stay alive, but he knew in the end he would be killed. It seemed that the men who feared death the most and tried their hardest to prevent it, were usually the ones who were killed first. And so it was for Sergeant Richard Hughes. Although Hughes bravely fought through his fear for almost three months, in the end, he either made the wrong decision or his luck ran out.

*The capture of Hill 192 gave the Americans a tremendous edge as the war continued. They now had the high ground around St. Lo that allowed the First Division and segments of the Second Division to overrun the town by mid to late July. The Ninth Infantry Regiment and Busi's squad continued south toward the towns of Vire and Tinchebray. The Allies now had more than two million troops on French soil and the results were becoming apparent. The Second Division was to keep exerting pressure on the German Seventh Army to the south and east and to push the enemy completely out of the Normandy Peninsula. General Omar Bradley was now ready to complete the breakthrough out of Normandy.

*(Source: *Combat History of the Second Infantry Division in World War II, 1946*)

Chapter 5
Snipers
July 21st - August 7th

On or around the 21st of July as Company D was advancing again through the last of hedgerow country, one particular hedgerow became a particular problem for Busi and the Second Squad.

Busi and his squad had taken up positions along the back of a hedgerow and waited for the riflemen of Company D to forge ahead on the right flank of the hedgerow (S.O.P was for the riflemen to move ahead of the machine gunners and secure the way for the rest of the Company to move forward). As the riflemen began to move up a small dirt road which was lined with trees and ran perpendicular to the hedgerow, shots could be heard coming from somewhere behind the next hedgerow.

One by one a sniper was picking off riflemen as they tried to move between the trees lining the side of the road. Busi watched over the top of his hedge and saw the riflemen being wiped out as they tried to advance. Finally, after seven or eight casualties, the riflemen retreated back to the hedgerow where the Sergeant and the rest of the Second squad were waiting to advance. They were totally confused as to where the shots were coming from. As one rifleman sat down next to the Sergeant, Busi could see the frustration in his face.

"They're killing all of us Sergeant…and we can't seem to find out where the hell they're at." The Buck Private confessed to Busi.

"Every time we try to move between the trees they know exactly where we are." he continued.

"You stay here. Red, come with me." The Sergeant ordered.

"Yes Sergeant." The rifleman seemed relieved.

Busi and Red grabbed their rifles, got up and started down the same road as the riflemen.

Private Red Clayton was a very large man. Six feet five inches tall with red hair and a huge build. He had joined Busi's squad just after D-Day as a replacement and was a good soldier. Good enough to still be alive after just a few weeks in battle, which was quite an accomplishment for a replacement.

As the two men moved up the tree-lined road, they passed the eight corpses of the riflemen shot dead just minutes before. Red began to get angry. As Busi moved behind each tree he was aware that no shots were being fired at him or Red. Had the sniper retreated to snipe another day? Why no shots? Busi, with Red right behind him continued up the road moving quickly, staying as low as possible and moving quickly from tree to tree until the two had reached the next hedgerow.

"I think he's gone Red." Busi whispered to Red.

"I hope not...I want his ass." Red snapped back.

"Let's move up on this side of the hedgerow and see if there's anything there...and keep low." Busi again whispered to Red.

The two men crouched low and began moving laterally across the hedgerow. The rest of the First and Second squads watched from behind the last hedgerow as the two men made their way along the hedge. About one-third of the way across the men were shocked and caught completely by surprise as the German sniper leaped out two-feet in front of them from a hole in the hedge.

"*No shoot...No shoot...No shoot!*" the sniper screamed as he popped out from inside the hedge with his hands on his head.

The two Americans were flabbergasted and quickly brought their guns up to shoot the enemy. Busi realized quickly that he was surrendering but Red wasn't impressed. *"God damn son of a bitch! Scared the livin' shit out me!"* Red screamed at the German Soldier.

Red took the butt of his gun and rammed it into the face of the sniper. The sniper fell to the ground as blood spurted from his mouth and nose.

"You rotten bastard...I'm gonna' shoot your ass right here." Red was hot.

Busi grabbed Red's gun by the barrel and shoved it toward the sky.

"No Red...Captain Hancock is watching back there...don't do it." Busi warned the Private.

Red again aimed at the sniper as he lay on the ground.

"He killed eight of our guys Sergeant." Red tried to convince Busi.

"I saw our guys too Red, but you shoot him now and Hancock will have you court marshaled. As much as I hate him, he gave up…you shoot him and you're in trouble." The Sergeant said, half whispering.

"You're right Sergeant." Red said.

"But this son of bitch deserves to die. He continued pointing his gun at the petrified German Soldier lying helpless on the ground in front of both men.

"Let's get him back to Hancock and let him figure out what he wants to do with him…maybe he has some information we can use…C'mon Red let's go." Busi said nonchalantly, trying to divert Red's attention.

Red was still hot, but finally calmed down a little. He grabbed the enemy sniper by his uniform right behind the neck and began dragging him back to the American lines for interrogation. Red was so strong he dragged the sniper twenty feet before he got to his feet and began to walk on his own. Red prodded the enemy with the nozzle of his gun as they walked back to the safety of their hedgerow.

Sergeant Busi crawled up the side of the enemy hedgerow to the backside to see that the sniper had dug a hole completely through the hedgerow to the front and covered the hole with weeds to conceal his position. Busi surmised that when the sniper saw the riflemen withdraw he may have taken a break and left down his guard allowing him and Red to move up to his position without being seen.

Another lucky break for the Sergeant and he thought to himself what could have been if the enemy sniper hadn't been so careless. Busi made his way back to the safety of the American hedgerow and made the necessary report to Captain Hancock.

Sergeant Busi would never see Private Red Clayton again. After bringing the German prisoner back to headquarters, Private Clayton was reassigned. No reason and no warning had been given. He was just gone. As it was with several of Busi's men, they were with him one day and gone the next.

At daybreak on July 27th Busi and his men moved slowly along a small dirt road several miles from the town of Vire. The road came to an end and the Sergeant now was faced with the task of moving his squad through an open field that spread out in front of him for about two hundred yards.

At the other end of the field was a hill that offered the enemy a very big advantage if they were inclined to be there. Weeds several feet high gave good cover, but the crossing was fraught with danger. Mines, snipers and who knows what lie on the other side of the hill.

"Sultz." Busi shouted out.

"Yea Sarg?" Sultzaberger replied as he walked up next to the Sergeant.

"Me and you will take the point here but we all have to be on bellies across this field. I don't like hangin' our asses out for the whole German Army to see." Busi explained.

"Gotcha' Sergeant, you and me. Let's go." Sultzaberger replied.

Private Robert Sultzaberger joined the Second Squad on June 7th, and had known Sergeant Busi since basic training in Wisconsin. He was a good soldier and managed to survive the first five weeks of the war. Busi was happy to have him since experienced combat men were becoming harder to find.

The Sergeant and Sultzaberger entered the field and began crawling on their stomachs with their rifles cradled in their arms. As they moved further into the open the rest of the squad repeated the maneuver and all ten men were now moving through the open field with the weeds as their cover.

Busi and Sultz crawled almost to the far end when the Sergeant looked up and saw a German soldier standing at the top of the hill aiming his rifle right at him. The German squeezed the trigger and fired a round.

"Ping." the shot rang out as Busi covered his head with his hands expecting to be shot.

Much to his surprise he was not hit and as he again looked up he saw his enemy turn and begin running down the hill out of sight. Busi jumped to his feet and began to chase the sniper.

"Let's go Sultz. We got him on the run." Busi yelled.

Sultzaberger never moved. Busi looked back and saw Sultzaberger still lying in the weeds. He realized that the sniper probably hit Sultz and his quest to run down the Nazi took on an even more important meaning.

The Sergeant reached the top of the hill and saw his enemy running wildly across an open field at the bottom the hill a hundred yards away. He knelt down, lifted his rifle and put the enemy in his sights. Just then the German soldier turned and saw the Sergeant at the top of the hill. He stopped running, turned toward the Sergeant and grabbed his rifle off his shoulder but he was too late. Busi squeezed his trigger and the shot rang out. The German's hands sprang in the air as his rifle flew away from his body. Busi saw a small puff of dust emanate from the soldier's chest as the bullet pierced the enemy uniform and threw him backwards to the ground. The Sergeant watched and waited to see if there was any movement. There was none.

He sprang to his feet and ran down the hill cautiously approaching the sniper. As he came up on the sniper the Sergeant knew he was dead. He aimed his rile at the lifeless body just in case he was wrong. He used his rifle muzzle and poked at the sniper's dead body. There was no response. He saw his bullet hole and blood in the enemy uniform and knew that his shot was a perfect shot through the heart.

He looked at the face of the German Sniper and realized he was no more than nineteen or twenty years old. He knelt down next to the dead sniper and began rummaging through his pockets looking for some information. When he reached the left chest pocket of the uniform he pulled out a photograph. The picture was of the sniper with his young wife and infant baby all happily smiling.

For a moment he felt a tinge of sorrow and for the first time since the war began he actually felt something for his enemy. Suddenly, almost as if reality struck him in the head he remembered his friend Sultzaberger on the other side of the hill. His sorrow turned to instant hatred as he stood up and threw the photo on the ground next to the dead sniper.

"Fuck you, you son of bitch. You deserved to die you Nazi bastard." He mumbled to the dead soldier and began to run back up the hill.

As he ran over the crest of the hill he saw the squad gathered around Sultzaberger's lifeless body. He feared his friend was dead but somehow hoped he was still alive. As he approached the squad he saw a medic kneeling over Sultzaberger's lifeless body.

"He's gone, Sergeant." the medic reported as he stood up.

"Sorry, Sarge." he continued as he dropped his head.

Busi looked down at his dead friend and saw a bloody hole in his uniform just above his right shoulder. The bullet entered his shoulder and went right through his body.

The Sergeant didn't say a word. He knelt down next to the corpse, reached under the uniform and pulled out Sultzaberger's dog tags. He opened his friend's mouth, put one dog tag between his teeth and closed his lower jaw. He put the second dog tag in his own pants pocket and stood up.

The rest of the squad watched in complete silence as the Sergeant completed his grizzly duty.

The Sergeant's emotions almost got the best of him. He wanted to scream. He wanted to cry like a baby. He was so angry he gritted his teeth. He was filled with so much hate he wanted to kill the entire German Army, single-handedly.

He repressed it all. He slung his rifle over his shoulder and began walking up the hill. He turned his head around to see the shocked look on the faces of his squad.

"Let's go." he said in a quiet voice.

The men followed their hardened leader over the hill and past the dead Nazi who had killed the Sergeant's good friend. No words were spoken.

Private John Harrigan had been with the Second Squad since D-Day plus one. He was one of only a few original members of the Second Squad that remained. The constant flow of replacements and reassignments of men in Busi's Squad was troublesome for the Sergeant and it became very difficult to get to know any one soldier very well.

John Harrigan got to know his Sergeant very well as he fought along side him now for almost two months. Busi liked Harrigan and thought he was a good soldier. They stayed close in past battles and Harrigan watched out for his squad leader. Harrigan had seen the heroics of his Sergeant and thought highly of him. Busi returned the respect as Harrigan proved time and again that he was not only a good soldier, but he managed to stay alive this long.

As the two moved forward with the rest of the Ninth Infantry Regiment on the morning of July 28th, the Second Squad approached an old wooden French home on the outskirts of the small town of Vire. They were several hundred yards from the house as Busi gave the signal to his men to stay low and seek cover. The men spread out in the small field that stretched from their position to the front of the house.

"Take five fellas' then we'll see what's in that house." Busi gave the order as the men lay down in the high grass.

"Harrigan." Busi called to his friend.

Harrigan moved closer.

"That's me." Harrigan replied as if he were singing the words from the song.

"What do you think?" Busi asked.

"The house? I'll tell you what I think after we take our five Sergeant." Harrigan joked.

"I don't like it." The Sergeant had a sixth sense about these things as he eyed the structure.

Busi pulled his rifle off his shoulder and sat down in the high grass. Harrigan joined him, but laid down three feet away.

"Ping." a sniper shot rang out and Busi quickly sprawled face down on the ground next to Harrigan.

"I told you I didn't like that house." Busi said to his friend. There was total silence.

"*Harrigan.*" He shouted.

"*Harrigan...are you hit?*" Busi shouted louder this time.

He crawled on his belly over to his friend and saw blood trickling from Harrigan's mouth.

"*Oh shit Harrigan, where are you hit!*" Busi shouted as he

looked for a bullet hole and found none.

Harrigan looked at his friend, eyes wide open. He tried to speak, but no words came out of his mouth.

The Sergeant pulled off Harrigan's jacket to see a small bullet hole in his left shoulder that went straight through his body as he lay in the grass. Harrigan lay dying and there was nothing Busi could do.

"*Medic…Medic*!!" he screamed.

A medic from one of the other squads only a few hundred yards behind the Second squad came running toward the dying Private. It only took him a minute or two to reach Busi and the dying Harrigan but it was already too late.

"Where's he hit Sergeant?" the medic asked.
Busi had is hand covering the wound in Harrigan's shoulder.

"Right here." he pulled his hand away as the blood poured out of the wound.

The medic looked at Harrigan and put two fingers on his throat to get a pulse.

"He's gone Sergeant." He said to Busi as he pulled the Private's coat over his head.

"Sorry, Sarg…there's nothing I can do for him."

Busi was sick. One shot and Harrigan was gone. He lay there for several minutes in disbelief but his sorrow soon turned to hatred and anger as he thought about the Nazi bastards in that house. He couldn't bring back his friend, but he sure could do some damage to whoever killed him.

He quickly got his thoughts together and began to act. Normally, he would call for artillery to level the house and kill everyone in it by sending the coordinates back to the big guns, but this was personal.

"Son of a bitch." Busi mumbled as the medic began crawling back to his position.

He was focused on the house where the deadly shot had been fired. He knew that most likely the sniper was located somewhere on the second floor, taking advantage of the high vantage point to scout out the advancing GIs.

Instead of calling in the big guns to obliterate the structure

Busi took matters into his own hands. He quickly moved parallel to the front of the house toward the other two machine gun emplacements attached to his section. He jumped into the bunker with the two gunners lying behind their thirty-caliber Heavy.

"Corporal, get this gun to the right flank of that house and for Christ's sake keep low. I don't want any more casualties from that sniper. Wait for my signal and blast the shit out of that second story." He commanded the gunners.

"Yes Sarg." The number one gunner replied.

Busi watched as the two gathered their heavy and crawled across the weeded field to another bunker created by an artillery shell just to the right side of the house one hundred yards away.

He ran back along a parallel line to the front of the deadly house to set up the other two thirty calibers. The sniper opened up on the Sergeant as he weaved his way between the bunkers and sparsely spaced trees to get the guns set up. The sniper kept missing him to the backside and Busi knew this was probably not an experienced German sniper…probably another French sympathizer the Nazis convinced to commit a suicide mission. The Sergeant knew he should have been hit by now, and was creating a moving target for the sniper. No matter who it was, they would soon have the fury of one very upset Sergeant unleashed on their unsuspecting, misguided life.

Busi returned to his Heavy with his number two gunner. He jumped behind the gun and carefully aimed his sights on the middle of the three, second story windows. He squeezed the trigger and the thirty-caliber began to rip out pieces of the old wooden French house. As he began to shoot, the other two thirty-calibers began to spray the second story as well. Tracers were entering through all three windows and large chunks of house began falling as hundreds of thirty-caliber shells literally tore the second story wood building apart.

Busi knew that the thirty-caliber bullets would cut through the old wooden house like a hot knife through butter. With three machine guns positioned along the entire front and side of the house, there would be no escaping this onslaught. The three heavys continued to riddle the structure for well over a minute pumping several thousand rounds into the house. The second story began to cave in and several feet of roofing plummeted to the ground. The three guns reloaded and again began firing, this time at the first story just in case some smart ass thought he could escape. One more blistering minute of heavy fire totally obliterated what was left of the first story.

Busi's gun went silent and he gave the order to silence the other two Heavies. The Sergeant waited and watched the decimated structure to see if there was any movement. He listened for sounds inside the house and heard nothing. He could see daylight through the thousands of holes in the old wooden house and knew there would be no survivors.

He gave the signal for three riflemen on his right flank to circle the house and enter from the back or right side. He saw the men slowly approach the house in a crouched position and disappear around the back. Within several minutes of waiting he saw one of the rifleman appear at a destroyed window on the first floor, waving to the rest of the section. It was all clear.

Busi entered the house along with several other men to see what was left. On the second floor there were two dead French civilians, almost unrecognizable, from the hale of thirty-caliber bullets. They were still clutching their German made sniper rifles as if they were going to use them again. On the first floor there was another dead French Civilian whose body was also torn apart by the deluge of gunfire from the Americans. He too was still clinging to the German rifle.

As Sergeant Busi and his squad surveyed the results of their devastation, he felt a sense of pleasure and joy, unlike June 7th and the woman sniper earlier in the war. He had seen so much death and destruction in less than two months of war that there was now a sense of satisfaction in killing the enemy…almost euphoria. Besides, these were the vermin who killed Harrigan and it gave him even more pleasure to see their lifeless bodies.

Although these were French civilians, it made no difference to him. When these misguided Frenchmen picked up a rifle and fired at the Sergeant or his men, they were the enemy…and they would suffer the consequences just as if they were Hitler's

Henchmen.

Busi congratulated his fellow GIs for a job well done. He coldly pried the rifle out of one of the dead Frenchmen's bloody hands and disabled the weapon so it could never be used again against him. Two other GIs did the same with the remaining dead enemy.

The Sergeant left the destroyed house and walked back to the body of his dead friend. He knelt down on one knee as he looked at Harrigan's face. He removed the dog tags from around his neck, placed one tag between Harrigan's teeth and slipped the other into his own pocket. He stared at his lifeless friend and shook his head.

"Why, Harrigan, why you?" he mumbled.

Busi stared at his friend for a few more seconds and before the knot in his stomach became unbearable he stood up and walked away in disgust.

Busi's squad watched the Sergeant as he got up and walked toward them. No words were spoken and the squad left the destroyed building and moved closer to the town of Vire, now less than a mile away. As they approached the sounds of war were everywhere and the smell of death was ever present.

Sergeant Busi had become an efficient killing machine and with each passing day of combat he was convinced that the more enemy he could kill, the sooner the Allies would win and the sooner he could go home. With the death of so many of his friends and fellow soldiers, the enemy had become an inanimate object to him. He knew that his enemies, given the chance, would slaughter him in an instant. He had become cold and calculating and viewed each enemy corpse as one more object that would not have the opportunity to kill him. The hatred for his enemy grew stronger and was the driving force that motivated him to kill every day.

The Second Division's job now was to maintain terrific pressure on the German Seventh Army that now found itself in constant retreat. The Americans were continuing to push the Nazi's south and east, completely out of the Normandy Peninsula.

The town of Vire had been almost completely obliterated as the Army Air Force had bombed the town prior to the Second

Division's entry. Now the job for Busi and his men was to enter the town and go house-to-house clearing each street of snipers and what was left of the retreating German Seventh. It was extremely hazardous since the advancing GIs had no idea where the enemy was hiding.

Within a few days the task was completed and the Ninth continued to force the German War Machine to retreat.

Busi's squad had suffered many casualties including several of his closest friends. Private Eldon Davis who the Sergeant had known since basic training was killed on August 3rd as the Second Squad attempted to secure the town. As replacements continued to take the place of the dead, the Sergeant became more and more hardened.

He would not let himself get close to his new replacements and in many instances didn't even know their names. He knew they probably wouldn't be around very long and getting to know them would only make it harder on him when they were killed.

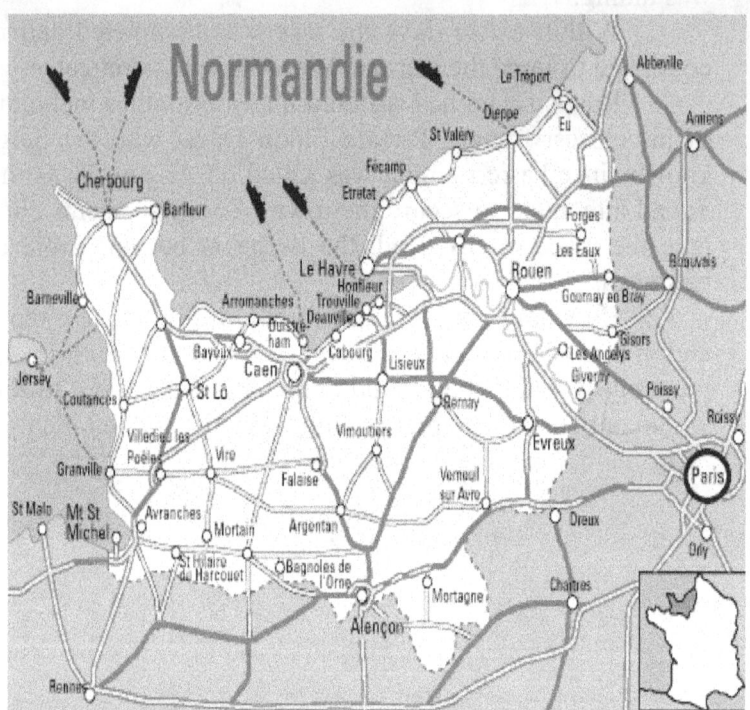

Map of Normandy Region of France. St. Lo and Vire are visible left center area of map
Map by Google Images

Chapter 6
The Messerschmitt and the Bronze Star
August 8th – August 16th

The Second Division marched on southeast toward the town of Tinchebray. On August 8th the Ninth Infantry moved into position to relieve the Twenty-Ninth Infantry outside the town. Sergeant Busi and the men of the Second squad dug their foxholes for the night. Busi was settled in his foxhole that was positioned next to a Willys Jeep that had been rigged with a thirty-caliber machine gun mounted in the rear.

This gun was fixed to a long support arm and actually stood up about four feet above the floor of the Jeep. It allowed the gunner to traverse the gun at steep angles needed to fire at approaching aircraft. Day light was waning on the evening of August 7th and Busi had just closed his eyes for a few minutes of much needed rest when he heard the sound of a small aircraft engine whining somewhere above his head.

Busi didn't give it a second thought. Just another spotter plane he thought to himself as he also thought about PFC Cook a recent replacement now positioned on watch at the gun in the Jeep. The Air Corps used small single engine Piper Cubs as spotter planes to fly over enemy lines just above tree level to survey enemy positions. It was a dangerous mission and many pilots were shot down because of the slow speed of the plane and it's incessant droning engine.

Just about to fall asleep, Pvt. Cook literally came flying in Busi's foxhole, covering his head and crouching low almost on top of his Sergeant.

"Cook, what the hell are you doing?" Busi shouted as he awoke from his stupor.

"There's a Messerschmitt chasing that spotter and he flew right over us!" Cook screamed as he covered his head with his hands.

Busi must have been totally asleep and didn't hear the

German fighter overhead. He grabbed his helmet, scrambled out of his hole and jumped into the back of the Jeep.

He could hear both planes now and the Cub was trying to escape the viscous guns of the Messerschmitt dodging in and out of the trees. The fighter dove almost vertically, blasting its guns at the helpless Cub. As the Messerschmitt leveled off it began another swing over Busi's head and made a right turn just above the tree line. Busi grabbed the handles of the thirty caliber and followed the fighter in the sights of the gun. His intensive training as a machine gunner again kicked in. He peered into the gun sight and moved the sight slightly forward of the Messerschmitt and pulled the trigger. The gun blasted out hundreds of rounds of thirty caliber bullets as the Sergeant followed the fighter in his sights. He watched as the tracers found their target right into the body of the German Fighter.

He riddled the Messerschmitt for thirty seconds as it screamed across the treetops. Smoke began to billow from the engine and trail behind. He continued firing until he lost sight of the fighter as it began to sink below the trees just a few hundred yards away. In an instant he heard a huge explosion and a tremendous plume of smoke erupted from behind the trees. He had downed the enemy fighter! Pvt. Cook crawled out of the foxhole in amazement. He had witnessed the whole incident from the safety of the hole.

"Holy shit Sergeant! I don't believe it." Cook blurted out.

The two GIs watched as the Cub continued on its flight in relative safety and out of sight.

Within minutes the two soldiers saw a Jeep driving toward them with Captain Hancock in the passenger seat.

"Oh shit, I'm in trouble now." Busi said quietly to Cook.

He thought the Captain would be furious with him for possibly giving away their position with all the firing. He never thought about that fact when he instinctively jumped on the gun to save the Piper Cub.

Hancock's Jeep approached the two men and skidded to a stop. Busi and Cook came to attention as the jeep approached.

"Who was doing the firing at that Messerschmitt, Sergeant?" Hancock asked sternly directed at his Sergeant.

"It was me, Sir." Busi admitted.

"I don't believe I've ever seen anything like that Sergeant. Good God that was great shooting!" Hancock said.
Hancock had also witnessed the whole incident from another vantage point.
Busi was relieved that his Captain wasn't upset with him.
"Thank you, Sir. I'm glad the Cub got away."
"You saved a lot more than that Cub. That fighter came out of nowhere. Took us all completely by surprise. Saw the whole thing from C.P. back there." Hancock said as he pointed toward the back of his Jeep.
"Damn good shooting, Sergeant...should have known it was you." Hancock said.
"Yes Sir!" Busi replied.
"Get some rest...we'll be moving out in the morning...and keep watch. There are reports of snipers in the area." Hancock commanded.
"Yes Sir." Cook and Busi both responded.
Hancock's driver turned the Jeep around and headed back to the command post.
The Sergeant slipped back into his foxhole for some needed rest, not really concentrating on his latest episode to foil the Nazis.
"Keep your eyes open Cook...you heard the Captain. Wake me in two hours." Busi said firmly.
"Yes Sergeant." Cook responded as he climbed into the Jeep and behind the thirty-caliber.
"Man, that was something else." Busi heard Cook mumble to himself as he settled in behind the gun.
Busi and Cook rotated two hour watches as the night of August 7th past without any further incidents. Replacement Private William Cook would be dead less than a week later on August 11th from wounds received during the battle of Tinchebray.
On August 8th Captain Hancock requested a Bronze Star Citation for Sergeant Joseph Busi for bravery under fire and the shooting down of the German Messerschmitt.
*NOTE: On August 16, 1944, the Second Infantry Division set a long-standing record. In World War I, the Division set a record of 56 consecutive days of fighting. That mark was eclipsed

as the Second's combat soldiers logged 70 straight days of front-line action, from D-Day plus 1 to D-Day plus 71. The weary soldiers of the Second Infantry Division finally were pulled back for a well-deserved rest and for the first time since D-Day they no longer had the enemy to its front. *(Source: *Combat History of the Second Infantry Division in World War II*, 1946)

The respite would not last long. The Division that had fought so hard through hedgerow country would now embark on three hundred mile journey to the City of Brest.

As mid August approached the American First Army split their Divisions. After successful campaigns at St.Lo and Vire the First Division (The Big Red One) headed east flanking the British Forces on their quest to liberate Paris. The Second Division now headed west toward the strategic port city of Brest. Although the Battle of Brest was ominous the journey to Brest was long and fraught with danger. The Ninth Infantry Regiment would suffer heavy losses and Sergeant Busi's Second squad was no exception. Busi would lose all but 3 of his men on the road to Brest.

The Germans knew that the City of Brest was important to their war effort and that it must be held at all costs. If critical seaports such as Brest, La Havre, Dieppe and Lorient were to fall, the Allies could use these points to lengthen their supply lines. The Germans would freely expend thousands of men defending these ports to make it difficult for the Allies to take. Brest was the most heavily defended of all these ports and the Second Division along with the Eighth and Ninth Divisions would need almost an entire month to get control of the seaport.

*The defense of Brest fell to German Commander, Major General Herman B. von Ramcke and 50,000 hodgepodge troops ranging in quality from the highly trained Second Parachute Division to postal employees and other civil servants. His mission was to occupy the Americans for at least 90 days because of the critical situation developing in the Fatherland. The German troops were told that every American shot fired in Brest was one less shot fired upon the Reich itself. Thus the German troops at Brest dug underground tunnels and made the American forces virtually obliterate the city, blasting every building within the city before they would surrender. In the end the Americans, of course, would prevail but with heavy casualties and a tremendous loss of equipment. *(Source: *Combat History of the Second Infantry Division in World War II, 1946.*)

Chapter 7
Fifteen Minutes of Fame
August 25th

As the Second Infantry Division marched west toward Brest there were periods of brief respites for the GIs, as well as peppered aerial attacks by the German Luftwaffe. The Americans were on the move and met some resistance as the German war machine was in full retreat, now split by Allied forces.

Busi and the Ninth Regiment, now very close to the City of Brest, rested on the side of a dirt road. Sounds of the Army Air Corps pounding the city could be clearly heard as a young Lieutenant approached the Sergeant.

"Are you Busi?" the Lieutenant asked.

"Yes sir." Busi replied.

"Come with me Sergeant…there's a reporter here that wants to interview you."

"Me Sir?" The Sergeant was stunned.

"That's right soldier. Word got around about what you did back in hedgerow country. We all heard about it. Your gonna' be on the radio all over the States!" the Lieutenant replied.

Busi, confused at this point, grabbed his rifle and headed back to a waiting truck that had several other soldiers sitting in the back. The other men were from various outfits of the Second Division who had received citations for heroic acts during the first few months of the war.

The truck pulled away and the ride took about ten minutes. As the truck came to a stop the men could see a small group of tents set up with several antennas connected. Busi had no idea what this was all about, but he was about to find out.

"This is it boys." The Lieutenant called out as he walked toward the back of the truck.

"Just head back to that tent and Mr. Hicks will tell you what he needs." The Lieutenant pointed to one of the tents with the antennas.

Busi jumped from the truck and headed for the tent. As he approached with the other men a man with large horned rimmed glasses immerged throwing the tent flap back. He was clean-shaven and neatly dressed, unlike the doughboys he was about to interview.

George Hicks was the London Bureau Chief for the "Blue Network" one of two networks owned by N.B.C. at the time (the Blue Network eventually became A.B.C. in 1945). He was hosting a program called "Victory Parade of Spotlight Bands" sponsored by the Coca Cola Bottling Company and was in Europe to interview some GIs. It was a campaign to drum up support for the war by showing how the troops were performing heroic acts and beating back the Nazis.

Hicks made history earlier in the war by reporting the D-Day invasion of Normandy live from the deck of a U.S. naval ship while under attack from Nazi warplanes.

"Afternoon boys. My name is George Hicks and I'm here to talk to you about some of the things you boys have done over here. I'll go over my questions with you first, give me your answers and if everything is O.K. we'll go ahead and broadcast it back to England. Your interview will then be heard on 173 radio stations back in the States. Now how does that sound?" Hicks queried, not really expecting anyone to answer.

Busi spoke up.

"Mr. Hicks, I really don't want to do this." He declared.

"What's your name son?" Hicks pressed.

"Busi, sir."

"Are you Joe Busi who killed all those Germans and saved a bunch of your buddies with your thirty caliber between the hedgerows?" He asked.

"Yes sir...but I'd rather not talk about it." Busi replied.

"You're quite a hero, son... don't you want your mother to hear your voice and let her know what you did here?" Hicks asked.

"No, not really." Joe replied

"Ah come on Joe, let the people back home hear your story and let them know we're kickin' this enemy's butts...it'll be good morale for the folks and the troops! Hicks was really putting on the hard sell to the Pennsylvania boy.

"Yea, I guess it couldn't hurt." Joe finally agreed.

"That's the spirit. Why don't you go first Joe...come on in and we'll talk." Hicks said as he grabbed Joe by the arm and lead him inside.

He turned to the other three GIs.

"Relax boys. Have a seat...smoke 'em if you got 'em. It won't be too long." Hicks reassured them.

Joe walked in and sat down across the table from Hicks. There was a microphone and some recording equipment on the table. He removed his helmet and placed his weapon on the floor next to the table.

This all seemed very strange to the Sergeant since he had been sleeping in holes, eating K-Rations and being shot at for the past ten weeks. He was tired, dirty and for the first time in over two months he realized he smelled like one of his hound dogs back in Edri, Pennsylvania. It didn't matter. It felt good to just relax, even if it was just for a few minutes.

"Joe, I have the report on what happened back at that hedgerow so I'll ask you some questions about that day and just answer my questions. O.K.?" Hicks asked.

"Yea. I guess." He replied.

Hicks turned on the recorder and set up the interview by describing whom he was talking to and what the situation was at the hedgerow. He asked his first question.

"So the Germans knocked out a Sherman Tank and then what happened Joe?" Hicks asked.

"Yea, those Goddamn square heads..."Joe started.

"Whoa Joe." Hicks interrupted. "You can't curse on the radio... just don't use any curse words, O.K.?"

"Yea, O.K."

"Go ahead, Joe." Hicks continued.

"Yea, those square heads had us pinned down..." Joe continued.

"Joe...Joe" Hicks interrupted again. "You can't use the words 'square heads.'

"Why not? Square heads, hinnies, krauts, jerries, fuckin' Nazis…that's what we call them, *God damn it!*" Busi was getting upset.

After two plus months of being shot at, Busi was in no mood for this. If this guy wanted a true picture of what happened he was going to hear the straight scoop and the boy from the backwoods was not going to tone down his words for an interview he didn't really want to do. Besides, he thought, he probably wouldn't make home alive anyway so who cares.

Hicks realized he was talking to a hardened combat soldier that had bigger things to worry about than what someone back home thought about him for using an ethnic slur.

"OK Joe, just don't use any curse words." Hicks said trying to calm the Sergeant down.

The interview continued and Hicks asked all about the hedgerow incident. Busi responded in great detail about how he had picked up the thirty caliber and blasted away at the enemy.

The interview lasted three minutes and forty seconds and by the end of the interview Busi had Hicks calling the Germans "hinnies" and "Jerries" in his interview questions.

When the interview was over the tape went back to England that same day with Hicks. It was broadcast on one hundred, seventy-three radio stations from coast to coast on the Blue Network of N.B.C. and it's affiliates at 9:30 P.M. (E.S.T.) on Friday, August 25, 1944.

Joe's mother heard the broadcast and was presented a shellac disc of the recording by the H. Repine of the Coca Cola Bottling Company of Indiana (PA.).

By the time the recording was played in the States, Busi was back with his outfit and back in battle…for the morning of August 26th had dawned in Europe and it would be yet another gruesome day for the men of the Ninth Infantry Regiment.

*Note: The heroic incident and the interview were both covered in several newspaper articles. In those articles they referred to Busi as P.F.C. Joseph Busi, but in actuality he had already been promoted to buck Sergeant.

Don Busi

*Field interview with George Hicks (London Bureau Chief for N.B.C. Radio), August 25, 1944 outside of Brest, France. Sponsored by the Coca Cola Bottling Company, N.Y., N.Y. Recording available on C.D. from Author.

Chapter 8

First Squad Annihilated
August 26th - A Horrible Day

August 26, 1944 is a day that Sergeant Busi will never forget. The village of Kermao, a small village on the outer ring of Brest, was ordered leveled by Second Division artillery because of the stiff resistance the Ninth Infantry was facing. For two days the Regiment tried taking the village to no avail. The Germans were dug in their fortified pillboxes and employed self-propelled eighty-eight millimeter guns and mortars to repel the advancing Ninth.

At 0800 hours (8:00 AM) the Americans began a massive twenty-minute long heavy bombardment, virtually obliterating the small town. Sgt. Busi's Second squad and Sgt. Luther Bone's First squad waited in their holes for the artillery to stop. They were to jump off immediately after the shelling stopped and try to advance on a hopefully disorganized and shattered enemy. Busi and his men were positioned to the left flank of Bone's First Squad, each man crouching in his own foxhole waiting for the order to attack. Bone on the other hand had all ten of his men in a large artillery hole that they used as a bunker and would all be jumping off together. This would prove to be a fatal mistake.

As the American barrage ceased, Sergeant Busi was ready to give the attack signal to his squad when he heard an incoming eighty-eight millimeter shell, a German response to the Americans. Busi ducked back into his hole seconds before he heard the shell hit seventy-five feet from his position. As he looked up from his hole to give the order again he saw a gruesome sight. The eighty-eight millimeter shell had landed directly in the middle of the First Squad. As the smoke cleared Busi could barely see what was left of the doomed squad. They never had a chance. As the German artillery rained more shells into the American lines, Busi jumped from his foxhole, gave the arm signal to his men and screamed the command to move out.

"*Let's go! Lets go!*" he shouted as he waved his right arm to his men to move out of their holes and advance.

As the men of the Second squad jumped off and began advancing, the Sergeant ran over to his right flank and jumped into the bunker that housed the First Squad. What he saw sickened him as he looked around the bunker. Sgt. Bone lay face down. The right half of his body was blown away by the blast. Busi dropped his weapon and undid his pack as he moved over to his long time friend P.F.C. Ross Wright who had been with Busi since basic training at Fort Sam Houston, Texas...almost two years.

"Medic! Medic!" Busi shouted toward the back lines for help.

Wright was sitting upright on the side of the bunker, helmet blown from his head that was slumped forward and bleeding, holding both his arms across his abdomen. As Busi picked up Wright's head he saw that he was still alive.

Wright looked at his friend and began moving his lips as if to say something, but no words came out of his mouth. The Sergeant pulled Wright's arms away from his body and saw his entire abdomen had been sliced open by shrapnel. His bloodied intestines fell out from his wound and settled on his lap. Busi tried frantically to push them back into his body cavity but it was an impossible task. Sweat dripped out from under his helmet and onto his patient as he quickly reached inside his pack and pulled out the standard issue bandage along with a can of sulfur powder. He sprinkled the powder on the bloody mess that was now Wright's abdomen and wrapped the bandage around his body to try to keep his intestines from falling out again. It only half worked. Most of Wright's intestines came back out oozing from around the bandage. The Sergeant again pushed what he could back into Wright's abdomen and positioned Wright's arms around his stomach to hold them in place.

"Hang on Ross...the medics will be here...just hang on." Busi said trying to reassure his dying friend.

Wright continued to look up at him but still couldn't speak. Busi just stared back at him in disbelief, knowing he could not stay by his side any longer. He began getting sick to his stomach as he realized that his good friend was dying.

As the German artillery continued to fall around him, he looked around the bunker and saw the other nine men of the First Squad and thought they were all dead. Body parts and blood were everywhere. He heard a moan from P.F.C. Addis, another close friend, who lay on the opposite side of the bunker from Wright. Addiss' left arm was blown completely off and blood gushed from his shoulder. He rushed over to Addis and pulled another bandage out of his pack and wrapped it around the Private as he moaned and grabbed at Busi with his right hand.

"God Damn it. Jesus, Addis hold on. The medics will be here." Busi said, now trying to convince himself that his two long time friends were going to be all right.

Busi could not stay any longer. The battle raged on and his men were trying to advance...he had to go *now*. No medics had arrived yet and probably wouldn't come until the battle pushed forward. There were plenty of wounded and it would be a busy day for the medics of the Ninth Infantry Regiment. He jumped out of the bunker leaving his long time friends to die a miserable, lonely death. But he realized that he didn't have time to think about the First Squad. If *he* was to survive, he had to think about what was happening now.

As he ran from the bunker machine gun fire zipped passed him and an unending barrage of mortar shells exploded around him. This was as bad as it got. He continued to move forward and caught up with the rest of the Second Squad, only to see that there were many casualties. The assault ground to a halt on the outskirts of Kermao as the German resistance was too much for the Americans. Unable to move any closer through the deluge of eighty-eights and mortar fire the Second Squad and the rest of the Ninth was ordered back to their original positions.

As the Sergeant fell back he made his way to the fatal bunker that had claimed the lives of the First Squad and in passing saw P.F.C. Wright slumped over face down at the bottom of the bunker... dead for sure. This was confirmed in his mind now because he also noticed that P.F.C. Addis was gone. The medics did in fact make it to the doomed squad and took him back, leaving Wright and the other eight dead GIs. Busi was on the run and could not stop at the decimated bunker, but merely ran by and observed the bloody mess again. Mortar shells and machine gun fire continued to blast away at the Second Squad as they made their way in retreat.

The heavy American artillery fire failed to dislodge the Germans dug in at Kermao. After yet another attempt to overrun the Germans, Busi and the Ninth Regiment were again pushed back, this time past their original jump off position, incurring heavy casualties. Busi lost another three men, recent replacements, in just this one surge alone. These losses and the loss of the entire First Squad was almost too much for the Sergeant to comprehend.

By 1300 hours (1:00 PM) on August 26th the Ninth Infantry Regiment lost some two hundred yards beyond its line of departure and incurred many casualties.

Sergeant Busi dug his foxhole for the night and as he settled in his hole he thought about his good friends Bone, Addis and Wright. He wondered if Addis was still alive. Bone and Wright were gone now and he thought back to boot camp where he met both men. He thought about how they became his close friends. He went on leave with them in the States, had fun in Ireland before D-Day, ate, slept and fought with them. The war was over for them now but he had to carry on. He continued to ask himself the same haunting questions and at times even asking God.

"Why am I still alive? So much death around me and yet I am still here. Why? When will it be my turn and how will it happen? Maybe I'll get it tomorrow, maybe the next day, maybe next week? Are Bone and Wright better off than me?" These questions continued to ring inside his head as he fell asleep in his hole. He hated this war.

It would take another two days for the Ninth Infantry to overrun the stubborn German defenses at Kermao and on August 28th the Ninth finally moved their Command Post to the bombed out forward positions that once was the Village of Kermao.

P.F.C. Addis had indeed survived, as Joe would find out after the war. The medics moved forward after the push off and saved Addis from bleeding to death. Busi would never see Addis again.

Sergeant Luther Bone was killed instantly that day as the

eighty-eight millimeter shell exploded and ripped his body in half.

P.F.C. Ross Wright died of his wounds despite the frantic efforts of his friend to save him. P.F.C. Ross Wright is buried at the American Cemetery in the small town of St. James, Brittany, France, just fifty miles from where he landed on June 7th 1944, two and half months earlier. The other seven men of the First Squad, some recent replacements, were also killed instantly as the artillery shell found its target.

NOTE: At a Second Division Reunion some fifty-five years after the War, Joe was told by Capt. Ernst that the artillery shell that landed in the bunker of the First Squad was actually a shell from friendly fire…American Artillery from the Second Division. The U.S. Army has never confirmed this information.

P.F.C. Ross Wright
Killed in action near Brest, France. August 26, 1944.
Photo courtesy of John Wright.

Chapter 9

Unbelievable Luck
August 28th – September 19th – Brest, France

By August 28th it became apparent that the siege of Brest was going to be difficult and bloody. The Germans were instructed by Hitler to fight to the last man and that surrender was not an option.

In three days of fierce fighting the Ninth Regiment had advanced only a scant three hundred yards south of the Brest Airfield after taking the Village of Kermao. The enemy was well-coordinated and maintained heavy pressure on the advancing American Forces making it extremely difficult to break through their defensive positions.

Early evening on August 28th Busi and his squad had been ordered to dig in for the night after a day of unflinching attacks and counterattacks. Almost completely exhausted Busi finished digging his hole and was about to climb in when he remembered seeing a small stack of hay in a field not far from his hole. How nice, he thought, to have a little hay in his hole to comfort his ragged, aching body! He grabbed his rifle, slung it over his shoulder and made his way to the field only one hundred yards or so to his rear. He saw the hay pile and began to make his way toward it when something caught his attention out of the corner of his left eye…something was moving and it was on the ground.

He quickly swung his rifle off his shoulder and knelt down on his left knee, bringing his rifle into firing position. It was dusk and very difficult to make out shapes as the light of the day began to wane. He didn't move and concentrated on what looked like a body lying on the ground twenty yards away…and it was moving. Was it an enemy soldier crawling toward him?

The Sergeant stared at the body and was now totally fixated on the mass moving on the ground. It was moving but it wasn't going anywhere. He stood up and moved slowly toward the body, gun up and pointed right at it. As he got to within ten feet it became all to clear what had given the Sergeant so much concern. As he walked up on the body the smell overwhelmed him. He began to dry heave and turned his head away. There in front of him was a dead GI, obviously killed days before. The body rotting in the hot August sun for days appeared to be moving from the millions of maggots that ate his flesh and produced an odor like none other.

Busi could get no closer. The smell was unbearable and the maggots made him sick. He quickly moved away in disgust and headed for the haystack. He mumbled to himself and grimaced at what he had just seen. He shook his head in disbelief.

"Oh Jesus…help me! He pleaded.

Every time he saw the ravages of war, especially dead American Soldiers it made him angry and instilled a hatred of the enemy. This motivated him on a daily basis to kill the enemy…without hesitation, without remorse, to a point of total disregard for his own survival. He had become fanatical about killing as many of the enemy as he could!

He grabbed an armful of hay and made his way back to his hole for the night. He placed the hay in the bottom of the four-foot hole and crawled in. It was almost dark now and he was just about to remove his helmet when all hell broke loose.

Machine gun fire rattled from his right flank from his gunner and rifle fire broke out all around him. His adrenalin kicked in and he peeked up out of his hole just enough to see what was happening. He saw a German patrol of eight soldiers scrambling in all directions as they accidentally stumbled into the American lines and a firefight ensued. He grabbed his rifle and shot two enemy soldiers as they ran directly at him, as surprised as he was when he popped up from his hole. They fell dead not thirty feet from his hole. The firefight lasted several more minutes as Busi's Second Squad wiped out the rest of the unsuspecting German patrol.

After a few more minutes there was total silence. With barely enough daylight, Busi and several men from the Second Squad got out of their holes and made sure that all eight enemy soldiers were dead.

Busi climbed back into his hole hoping there would be no further incidents that night. He sat down at the bottom of his hole on the hay he had collected and removed his helmet. He moved around a little to try to get comfortable.

What he saw next froze him solid. A bullet hole in the front of his helmet had come not more than a half-inch from the top of his head. The bullet entered the front of his helmet, went all the way through, between the liner and the top of the helmet. There was a small hole in the back where the bullet exited.

He had been so focused on the firefight that he never realized that a bullet was less than an inch from blowing a hole in his head! He sat there for several minutes starring at the doomed helmet and thought about what could have been.

"Holy shit!" He whispered clearly to himself.

He continued to stare at the front of his helmet as he stuck his forefinger through the hole. He shook his head and pondered to himself.

'This is unbelievable…how could I be so lucky?' He thought.

'There is no way this could continue…it's just a matter of time…it's getting closer and closer!' he thought some more.

The daylight was gone now and he laid back in his hole continuing to think about the incident. He prayed to his Savior that he would be delivered from this evil and he would live to see his family again as he had done many times before this day. He knew the odds were against him, but he tried to think positively. If he could just make it through the next battle he might be able to make it. He struggled with thoughts of how unlikely it would be for him to get through this and the conflict inside him continued.

All was quiet now and he drifted off to a light sleep. The sounds of war continued in the far distance as he dozed off. There were no further incidents that night, and the Sergeant slept lightly.

After almost three months of intense combat deep sleep was impossible. Infantry soldiers on the front lines of the war could not afford to sleep too deep. They were always on edge with an ever-present enemy. A GI who slept too deep could find himself with an enemy combatant on top of him in the middle of the night ready to slit his throat. So the GIs slept with one eye open and aware of the slightest noise around them.

As dawn broke, Busi climbed out of his hole and was informed that his platoon had orders to fall back and get some hot chow and maybe a shower. He was ecstatic. He smelled like one of his farm animals, with no change of socks or underwear for at least six weeks and the same K-rations were getting old.

The Second Squad pulled back and several trucks picked up Busi and his men and drove a mile or so to the rear where there were some makeshift kitchens and some tents for showers set up.

The Sergeant jumped down from the back of the truck and moved to a line of GIs that had formed in front of some tables set up with huge steaming pots. The food looked good and as he approached the first table he saw First Sergeant Babin behind the table serving food to the troops.

"Hey Sergeant." Busi greeted Babin.

Babin looked up from a steaming pot and spotted Busi.

"Sergeant…how are you?" Babin said with a smile on his face.

"Good…food looks good." Busi looked down at the food as he responded.

Babin's smile left his face as he saw Busi's helmet.

"Soldier, get that God Damn helmet off your head and get another one…what the hell is wrong with you?" Babin scowled at Busi.

Busi forgot about the hole in his helmet and remembered it was there when Babin ordered him to get rid of it.

"Yes Sarg." Busi responded.

He took the helmet off his head and tossed it on the ground. It rolled a few feet and stopped. He suddenly felt a tinge of sadness.

He looked at the helmet on the ground and thought that he would like to have kept it. He had some strange attachment to that helmet. It had been with him since D-Day and the bullet hole reminded him of the incredible luck he had had to this point in the war.

He knew someone with a higher rank would eventually make him get rid of the helmet. He knew why and thought the reason was ridiculous. A hole in a GI's helmet was bad for morale…especially for the green troops and replacements that hadn't seen much combat. It was demoralizing and scared the hell of the new guys. Imagine a green replacement seeing a hardened combat soldier right off the front line with a bullet hole through his hat! It was not very reassuring for the new guys.

Busi found this to be somewhat hypocritical since these replacements would soon find out what this was all about. Better for them to see the reality of the situation than try to give them a warm fuzzy feeling that everything was going to be fine. It wasn't going to be fine and more than half of them would probably be dead within a week.

He got his hot chow and sat down at one of the tables set up around the camp. He enjoyed the hell out of the eggs, potatoes and several pieces of white bread. He finished his meal and lay down under a huge Oak tree. It felt good to relax even though he knew it wouldn't be for very long. Sure enough, within the hour orders came to load up. It was back to reality and the war.

The Second Squad was returned to the front line of battle outside Brest and Busi and his troops returned to their holes.

The perimeter of Brest was surrounded by large hills and the Germans put them to good use. The Army Air Corps had been obliterating the city for several days, but somehow the German artillery continued to pound back at the Second Division ground troops.

The German War Machine had developed an ingenious artillery device that wreaked havoc on the Americans for several weeks on the outskirts of Brest.

In several strategic locations in the surrounding hills of Brest, (known as the "Outer Ring") the Nazis dug huge one-way tunnels into the side of the hills and placed railroad tracks inside the tunnels. The railroad tracks held flat –bed rail cars with huge artillery guns attached to the car. The gun could be rolled out of the hill on the tracks, drop shells on the advancing GIs and before the Air Corp could get there to destroy them, rolled back into the hill and out of sight. It was a hideous game of hide and go seek with deadly consequences for the American Second Division.

Sergeant Busi observed one of these beasts as his Second Squad made its way through the hills on the Outer Ring. The only way to defeat the large gun was to go around it and cut off the inhabitants until they gave up.

Fierce fighting continued as the Sergeant and his men made their way through the Brest Wall (the ancient wall that surrounded the inner city). Tenacious house-to-house fighting ensued and was extremely dangerous as the Germans surrendered only after every conceivable method of resistance failed.

Busi and his squad used all methods of close-in fighting to clear and secure the decimated buildings that were left standing by the endless Air Corp and ground artillery bombardments.

The city was decimated and on September 14th the three regiments of the Second Division moved forward against a determined enemy as troops continued to clear buildings one at a time. By the end of the day it was clear the Nazis were defeated in Brest.

The constant pressure of the Second Division on the Germans was so intense that as Busi and his squad moved from house-to-house German officers who were positioned in these homes literally were forced to make a hasty retreat with their warm dinners and French wine still on the kitchen table.

Finally, on September 19th after almost one month of constant fighting, German General Von Ramcke who had moved his headquarters across the Bay of Brest to the Crozon Peninsula surrendered to the Eighth Division. The General's objective, demanded by Hitler, of holding off the American Army for at least three months had been reduced to less than a month.

The spit-and-polish defeated German garrison, despite the intense bombing, was in sharp contrast to the disheveled and exhausted appearance of the victorious American troops. The American forces had been fighting since D-Day, through the French hedgerow country and finally through streets of Brest. Their appearance was somewhat less than neat.

Sergeant Busi lost another four squad members in the brutal battle for Brest, all of them replacements. Only Peepsight and the Sergeant remained as the original members of the Second Squad.

With the First Squad completely wiped out, only two GIs remained of the original eighteen men of the First and Second

Squads assembled on the beaches of Normandy on June 7th. The war was now three and half months old and nearly the entire First and Second Squads were either killed or wounded.

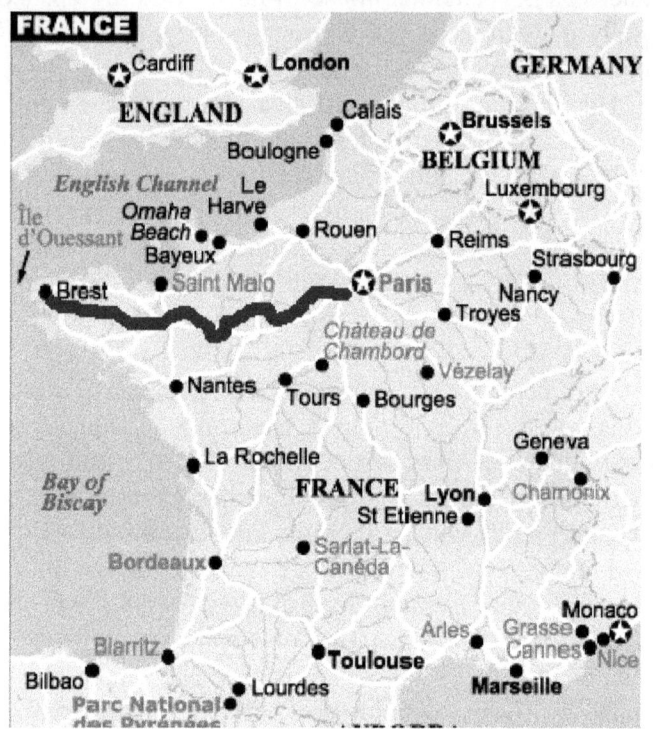

Map of France showing City of Best left center. Omaha Beach also shown.
Map by Google Images

Chapter 10

Ah! Gay Paris
September 26th – October 4th - Paris

After seven days of regrouping, reorganizing and just plain relaxing the Second Division was now ready to join the rest of the First Army that had split off earlier in the war and headed east. The First Division was already through Paris and positioned on the German Border just west of Aachen, Germany.

On September 26, Busi and his men boarded troop transport trucks twenty miles east of Brest and began the long journey to Paris.

The trip took three days as the transport trucks made their way through the French countryside on the "Red Ball Highway," the famed supply route to the Allied front.

Fifteen miles from the center of Paris Busi and his men jumped from the transport trucks and began their trek toward the City of Lights.

Sergeant Busi was in awe of the sights and sounds of the City of Lights but could not quite relax and enjoy the sights. After three and a half months of constant combat it was impossible for him to be let down his guard.

He actually was quite nervous, thinking a crazed Nazi sympathizer could take a snipe at him or toss a grenade into the middle of exposed Americans. He continued the trek down the famous streets of Paris that had seen the likes of Napoleon and more recently Adolph Hitler.

He marveled at the fact that the city was left unscathed by the war unlike the decimated remains of Brest and smaller towns like St. Lo and Vire.

The Germans had declared Paris an "open city". This meant that in the event of the imminent capture of the city, the German military that controlled the city would abandon all defensive efforts. The attacking Allies were then expected not to bomb or otherwise attack the city but simply march in. This declaration was aimed at protecting the historic landmarks and the civilian population from an unnecessary battle. And so Paris remained pristine.

Except for a few overzealous Parisians who probably had a little too much wine, there were no incidents. Busi and his men walked their way a few miles west of the city where Army tents and hot food awaited the weary Second.

The Sergeant settled in his tent and the supply truck that followed the Division east to Paris delivered his duffle bag that contained his personal belongings. He rummaged through it and found some paper and a pencil and finally took the time to write his mother. He always downplayed the danger and the horrors of war in his letters home so his mother would not worry too much about him.

Only he would carry the burden of the disturbing sights, smells and sounds of the unthinkable horrors of this war. Only he would know what it was really like. He thought about his family and the people of his hometown. How could they ever know and worse how could he ever describe this never-ending nightmare. None of that mattered and he only hoped he would see them again someday.

He finished his letter and procured a three-day pass to Paris where he and his friend Peepsight toured Paris like true tourists. After a few days he began to enjoy the sights and he actually started to unwind. Although sleep was intermittent at best, he ate some good food and drank a little French wine but always with a cautious eye.

The French welcomed the liberators wherever they went and it was not hard to procure a free bottle of wine or a true French meal. The doughboys soaked up the hospitality, but Busi realized that it would not last very long.

Upon returning to his camp on the outskirts of the city rumors were already flying that the Second Division was moving east to the German Border.

The Sergeant prepared for the move and he knew that within a few days his fun and relaxation would be a distant memory, as he would again be thrust into the front line of this miserable war.

Other rumors flew through the Division that the Germans were all but defeated and the war would probably be over by Christmas. The Sergeant wasn't buying any of it and he knew that anybody who thought the war was over was sadly mistaken.

On the morning of October 3rd, orders were given to the Ninth Regiment to move out. Busi and his men again boarded several transport trucks. When the trucks were full with men and equipment the convoy pulled away from the camp and headed east.

Chapter 11

A Thick Forest and Nowhere to Hide

October 4th – December 16th - Hurtgen Forest, Belgium

"I saw some of our guys cut in half by the tree bursts. A German artillery shell would whistle overhead and you just waited for it to hit the top of a tree. When it hit, shrapnel and chunks of tree would spray down on anything that was below, ripping it to shreds. I stood right next to the trunk of the tree to avoid being hit. I could hear shrapnel hitting six inches from my feet. After three days of constant shelling I thought I was going to lose my mind. You couldn't find anywhere to hide." Sergeant Joe Busi, 2005 interview.

"The Hurtgen Forest was the worst. If you didn't get your head shot off by the Nazi snipers and their burp guns, the tree bursts ripped you apart. The Germans slaughtered us. There were times when I had to shit and piss in my pants, because I knew if I stood up a burp gun would take my head off. We went in with a company of a hundred and fifty guys and were lucky to come out with sixty."
Sergeant Jack Derevensky (First Infantry Division) 2007 interview.

After the very brief respite in Paris, Sergeant Busi and the men of the Ninth Regiment were transported to the east along the Belgian-German border.

During the months of August and September while the Second Division was fighting in Brest, the rest of the Allies had pushed the Nazis east out of Paris and back to the Siegfried Line on the German Border.

The Siegfried Line was a defensive system stretching 392 miles south along the western German Border from the Netherlands to Switzerland. It contained over 18,000 bunkers, tunnels and tank traps built in 1938 by Hitler to keep any invaders out of the Fatherland.

Busi and his men quickly settled down and began to solidify their defensive positions and tried to feel out the strength of the enemy. Entrenchments and shelters were constructed and preparations were made for the coming cold weather.

Fighting in the area was relatively light during this period but patrols and enemy activity was always a concern for the Sergeant. Just north and east of the town of St. Vith, Belgium, Sgt. Busi and his squad were positioned in the dense Hurtgen Forest. This forest was part of a larger area known as the Ardennes that covered an area from Eastern Belgium to the City of Aachen, to the south and Luxembourg.

This heavily forested area was thick with trees and so dark, even during the day, that it made it almost impossible to see anything more than a few feet away.

The rains of fall and the coming winter made life in the forest miserable. Busi was constantly wet and his feet were so soggy that he feared the coming cold weather would give way to a condition known as "trench foot." This was a condition that developed when a soldier's feet were constantly wet, cold and in unsanitary conditions. If left untreated it could result in gangrenous feet and eventual amputation. Busi knew the only cure was to try to keep his feet dry and change his socks as often as possible.

It was not easy for him to carry out this procedure, especially since there was nowhere for him to dry his socks and removing his boots continuously, put him in grave danger with the enemy only a few hundred yards away. He managed to keep himself relatively dry and warded off the condition. Although he would suffer from a slight case of trench foot, his damage was limited.

The Sergeant and his men were now in a different kind of war. The day-to-day strains of combat in the hedgerows of Northern France were now replaced with the men holding in one place in a defensive position for many weeks at a time. Dangerous night patrols and short skirmishes with the Germans were the order of the day but no less stressful. Men were still dying while the top brass contemplated the Allies next move.

The standstill lasted for more than a month. Both sides planned their next move. Hitler had begun to assemble a massive strike force on the east side of the Siegfried Line and Eisenhower planned his strategy to enter The Fatherland. Every Allied soldier knew the German War Machine was not going to let the Allies waltz into their homeland. It would be a terrific struggle if the Allies struck first.

Busi and his men struggled against German patrols and the wet weather now turning colder as November approached. Since the Allies believed that the Germans were essentially defeated and the war would be over, winter supplies were not forwarded to the front lines. Winter coats and boots were not sent forward and as the weather got colder the Second Division was not prepared for the coming winter.

Hitler continued to fortify the Siegfried Line, knowing that it was now the only barrier to the citadel of the Reich. While Hitler continued to pour his troops on the western border, Eisenhower on the other hand had a very thin line of defense. This was especially true in the area of the Second Division. The twenty –five mile line they covered was four times the normal coverage for an Army Division and so vast that it was impossible to concentrate enough soldiers and adequately cover the border.

During this time, Sergeant Busi reported seeing several instances of German soldiers dressed in American uniforms capturing Americans and bringing them behind German lines for questioning. This was against the Geneva Convention and these Germans, when captured, were treated as spies and executed by firing squad. It was extremely underhanded and the Allies would have no part of it. Any enemy soldier caught in this act was treated in the most severe manner.

On or around October 29th as Sergeant Busi huddled in his trench hole in the early morning a soldier approached from his left flank. Busi, not sure who he was, aimed his rifle at the approaching soldier and commanded him to halt.

"Who goes there. Busi shouted.

"Private Joseph Popielarcheck, Eighty-Second Airborne. Are you Sergeant Busi?" the soldier replied.

"What's the password Private?" Busi demanded.

"Ah…brother!" the Private responded.

"I'm Sergeant Busi…Eighty-Second Airborne, what the hell are you doin' here?" Busi inquired.

"Well Sergeant I got separated from my outfit about a week ago and I've been trying to get back to them ever since. I guess I just don't know where they are at the moment. Anyway, I was sent to Captain Ernst and they're reassigning me to your outfit. The Captain said you could use me. I've had some training on the thirty caliber." He responded.

"How long you been over here Private?" Busi asked.

"Almost five months…right after D-Day." Popielarcheck sat down in the trench with the Sergeant.

"I guess you've seen some combat so that's good. Yea, I can use you. I'm going to put you with Peepsight as his first gunner. Just lost a replacement last week on patrol, so you can hook up with him. He's a good soldier so don't get him killed. We're the only ones left since D-Day and I'm very fond of him, understand?" the Sergeant said in a serious voice as he looked directly at the Private.

"Yes Sergeant, don't worry." Popielarcheck responded.

"Follow this trench. He should be three or four holes that way." Busi pointed to his right. "And stay low. The snipers here love to shoot people in the head!"

Popielarcheck smiled and nodded his head as he turned and began to move along the trench.

Private First Class Joseph Popielarcheck was quite stocky and originally assigned as a paratrooper with the Eighty-Second Airborne Division. He had been separated from his outfit a week earlier from an ill-conceived jump and ended up in the area of the Second Division. Since Busi was short several men in his squad, Popielarcheck was permanently assigned to the Second Squad and the Second Division. After a few weeks Busi had taken a liking to the Private. The Sergeant thought he was a fine soldier by the way he conducted himself in just the few short weeks he was with the outfit.

November 15, 1944 was a special day for Sergeant Busi. It was his birthday. As the day dawned he ascended from his hole in the forest and felt a little optimism about reaching his twenty fourth birthday. He did not tell anyone fearing the endless slaps on the back and constant reminders of how far he was from home on this day. As the boring day passed and his squad continued to stay in their defensive positions, only one thing was on the Sergeant's mind. Would he live to see his twenty-fifth birthday? The day ended just as the day before and no one was the wiser. He silently went about his business as if it were just another day…and in realty it was.

As November passed, each side maneuvered relentlessly to try and figure out the other side's next move and fall was now turning into winter.

On December 13, 1944 orders were given for the Ninth Infantry Regiment to begin an assault to the north of Malmedy, Belgium through the Hurtgen Forest. The green 106th Division, only on the European Continent for fifteen days, was to replace the Second Division as they moved north. The Second Division's objective was to capture the town of Aachen, a good-sized town about two miles inside the German border. The Nazi's had retaken Aachen as they pushed the Allies back across the Siegfried line in early November.

Busi and his squad prepared for the assault and began moving early on the morning of the thirteenth. As the soldiers of 106th began replacing Busi and his men, the Sergeant noticed that the unit was extremely young and very green. He shook his head and wished them good luck as the Second Squad moved out. He wondered how the green 106th would be able to hold their own against the experienced and hardened German War Machine just a few hundred yards to their east. Busi would find out later how correct his intuition was when the 106th Division was almost completely wiped out.

The entire Ninth Regiment was on the move and the trip through the forest began eerily quiet. Several hours passed and the Sergeant and his men moved slowly through the darkness of the trees.

Snow covered the ground and was several feet deep in some areas that made for slow going. Suddenly as if someone turned on a light switch all hell broke loose on top of the Second Squad and the rest of the Ninth Regiment. Heavy artillery began raining down on the foot soldiers and it was a horrific sight.

As the German artillery screamed overhead the eighty-eight millimeter shells clipped the tops of the seventy-foot pine trees and exploded in mid-air. This produced a tree burst explosion that sent shrapnel and tree limbs downward in a deadly shower of flying debris.

Sergeant Busi instinctively ran to the closest tree and stood as close to the tree trunk as possible, almost hugging it. The overhead explosions were terrifying as he hugged the tree trunk and watched as the deadly shrapnel sprayed down on the men of the Ninth Infantry. Some men were split in half as the downward spray shot through their bodies. Others had their heads and limbs sheared off as the flying debris sliced through them like butter.

The Sergeant seemed to think that the closer he stood to the trunk of the tree the less chance he had of getting hit with the downbursts. He surmised that the debris would spray outward from the explosion at the top of the tree and away from the trunk. He was partially right, but as he stood beside his tree he heard and saw shrapnel striking the ground all around him…not a good sign.

He began running from tree to tree advancing as quickly as he could to evade the tree bursts. It was terrifying and the Nazis were relentless with their barrage.

The Americans were trying to enter the Fatherland and they would pay a heavy price. The shelling lasted all day and the Second Squad was ordered to dig in and try to wait out the barrage, but it was futile. A hole in the ground would not protect the GIs from the downward tree bursts and many of Busi's replacements were mutilated just trying to dig a hole.

The Sergeant dug his hole close to a tree trunk and climbed in. He hoped the never-ending barrage of German eighty-eight shells would not hit his tree. He crouched at the bottom of his shallow hole and covered his head with his hands trying to make himself as small as possible. The shelling continued with blast after blast ripping the trees overhead and firing debris to the ground all around him. He began to tremble as he realized that there literally was no place to hide from these deadly explosions. Cries from the wounded and dying GIs cut to ribbons by the tree bursts were everywhere. It was difficult for him to listen to the terrible screams.

The barrage continued for hours and Busi's nerves began to wear down. He had been scared before…on the beach at Normandy and in the constant hedgerow fighting, but never like this. There was nowhere for him to go and nothing he could do to stop the artillery. He was helpless and at the mercy of his good luck and that made him more frightened.

The shelling continued into the evening and as night fell the Germans finally ceased their incessant bombing. Busi lay in his hole and for the first time all day began to calm down. Orders were given to stay in their holes for the night. Watches were set up as he would be on watch for two hours and sleep for two hours, but sleep was impossible…and so the night passed.

At daybreak Busi and his men again began to move through the forest and again all was fine for a few hours. As mid-morning approached the horror of the German Artillery began again. The closer they got to the German border the more intense the shelling became. The noise of the incoming shells and the tree bursts were almost too much to bear. Busi continued his tree-to- tree advances and his men followed him. Some were lucky and some were not. The shelling continued throughout the day and the casualties began to mount up.

The constant strain of the incessant shelling left Sergeant Busi an emotional wreck. Toward the end of the second day of tree bursts he could no longer withstand the stress. After two days of being completely on edge, the Sergeant began to lose control. He abandoned his tree-to –tree movement and sprinted to a small artillery crater covered with snow. Joe knelt down in the snow and took off his helmet. He used his helmet to begin digging a hole in the snow. Once through the snow, he feverishly dug into the half frozen ground with his helmet and then with his hands. As he formed a small hole in the side of the bunker he literally shoved his helmet-less head into the hole.

Although completely irrational, his thinking was clear. If a tree burst showered down shrapnel on him at least he wouldn't get his head ripped off. If the shrapnel hit his body, he may be able to recover. Better to get hit in the ass than in the head! His whole body trembled as he continued to kneel in the snow with his head hidden in the hole.

After several minutes with his head shoved in a hole, the Sergeant realized it probably wasn't a good idea to play ostrich in the middle of a war. He pulled his head out from the hole and by coincidence looked straight up to the top of the bunker. Standing at the top of the bunker looking down directly at him was Captain Ernst with shrapnel spraying down around him. Ernst looked at the Sergeant and began shaking his head side to side. A huge smile came over the Captain's face and he turned and walked down the opposite side of the bunker, without saying a word.

Busi's irrational stunt was somewhat amusing to his Captain and the Sergeant suddenly stopped shaking. Just the sight of his Captain fearlessly standing on top of the bunker with shrapnel raining down around him was enough to bring Joe back to reality. He put his helmet back on his head and regained his composure. He sat down in the snow and again tried to make himself as small as possible. Some time later the relentless shelling ceased and Busi and his men dug in for the night.

As the third day began it was more of the same as Busi and Ninth Regiment continued their advance toward Aachen. The shelling continued and more replacements in Busi's squad were killed by the unrelenting bombardment. Three more replacements were sent to the Sergeant to replace three other replacements that were killed the previous day. The deaths continued and today would be no different.

There was a brief pause in the barrage when Busi and his men came to a small clearing in the forest. As they approached the edge of the clearing they all saw an ominous sight. On the other side of the clearing was a German pillbox manned by no less than five Germans with several machine guns. The pillbox was a square three-foot thick concrete bunker with machine guns strategically placed in small two-foot wide by one foot high slits in the concrete.

They were imposing structures that struck horror in the minds of the Allied foot soldier. They were virtually impenetrable.

The Sergeant had cleared more than one of these horrors before and he knew the only way to kill the occupants was to use a flame-thrower from fairly close range. This was the only option and many times it would mean several American lives would be spent to ensure success.

The procedure was quite simple and Joe began to give the orders. Three men would approach the bunker head-on using whatever they could for cover. The first of the three men would carry the flame-thrower, which consisted of two tanks carried on the back and the long cylindrical thrower that shot a huge flame of flammable gas about fifty feet at the victims. If the flames hit the victim it was certain death that was quite agonizing as the victim burned. The remaining two men would follow behind and take over the equipment if the previous soldier was killed or wounded. The other five men in the squad would provide cover fire that would hopefully have the Nazi's ducking for cover as the flame-throwers made their way to the bunker. Unfortunately it didn't always go as planned.

Joe set up his cover fire and was the third man in the chain of flame-throwers to advance to the pillbox. He did not know the other two GIs since they were new replacements sent just the day before. Neither had experience with the weapon so they would now get on the job training.

The attack began as the Second Squad opened fire on the pillbox peppering the concrete structure with a hail of bullets. The three flame-throwers began to run through the opening in the forest toward the Germans. As they ran out of the woods in single file they bent themselves in half and tried to stay as close to the ground as possible. The foot of snow on the ground slowed their progress. The squad's cover fire caught the Nazis off-guard and they scrambled to man their guns.

A minute later the Germans opened fire toward the trees at the edge of the open field. As the barrel of their gun made it's way to Busi and his fellow GI's, the Sergeant tapped the man in front of him and the two men flew to the ground and into the snow. The number one man carrying the flame-thrower was not experienced enough to time his move and was caught with a spray of bullets from the German machine gun. He fell to the ground lifeless as Busi and the replacement helplessly watched. Several rounds whizzed over their heads as the German gun traversed the tree line.

The second replacement crawled up to the dead GI and began removing the flame throwing equipment. He checked to see if his comrade was still alive but a German round tore half his head off. The soldier donned the equipment as the German gun stopped firing. Busi crawled up behind his replacement and the second squad again started with cover fire. Busi and the replacement stood up and started toward the pillbox again.

The German gun opened up a second round of fire that traversed quickly across the landscape. As the gun made it's way to Busi and his fellow GI Busi again hit the ground but the replacement continued a few seconds too long. A bullet struck the GI in the chest and he fell to the snow. He moaned in pain as the Sergeant watched in disgust seething with anger as the Germans cut two of his men to shreds. Busi crawled up to the GI about ten feet from him and took the tanks off his back. He turned over the replacement to try to help him but he was already gone. The German gun had once again gone silent.

Joe was now close enough to use the deadly weapon so he placed the tanks on his back as he lay in the snow and grabbed the long metal shaft that threw the deadly flame. The second squad, observing from behind, again opened up with cover fire for their Sergeant. As the firing began Joe stood up and squeezed the trigger on the deadly weapon. Immediately, a huge flame of orange fire shot over fifty feet out of the barrel and the Sergeant aimed it directly into the small one-foot opening in the pillbox. A huge roar that sounded like a freight train filled the frozen Belgian air. He moved forward toward the pillbox cursing at the enemy inside. He was enraged at the loss of his squad mates and fearlessly made his way to the now burning pillbox. He relentlessly poured the liquid fire into the hole and flames began shooting out of the side holes in the bunker. He made his way to the front of the pillbox and continued saturating the fortress with fire.

He let go of the trigger and the flame-thrower went silent. He turned his back to the flames and leaned up against the side of the concrete bunker as he sat down in the snow.

He motioned for the rest of the squad to make their way to the bunker. As he looked at the slit in the pillbox that housed the German gun he saw that the barrel was tilted forward as if it had been abandoned. He also noticed something else. Silence. Usually the unfortunate victims in the pillbox would be screaming in agony as they were burning to death, but there were no such screams.

The Sergeant realized what had happened and quickly moved around to the back of the bunker as the inside burned. Just as he had suspected the enemy was long gone. After the last blast of machine gun fire the Germans sprayed at the Americans, they quickly vacated the bunker in fear of the inevitable. They moved quickly out the back of the bunker and disappeared into the wilderness.

Joe looked through the open door at the back of the bunker and saw nothing inside but flames. There were no scorched bodies or dead enemy anywhere. He was disgusted and threw the flame-thrower in the snow. After two straight days of constant shelling by the Nazis and now no enemy bodies to count, his self-control was running thin. He agonized over the dead replacements in combat for only one day. Replacements getting killed was commonplace, but their time in combat seemed to be getting shorter and it was beginning to get old for the Sergeant. There were just too many dead G.Is.

The rest of the squad arrived and checked out the empty bunker. Not much was said as they realized the terrible wasted lives of the two new replacements with no dead enemy to account for them.

The squad left the bunker and continued their advance toward Aachen through the Hurtgen Forest.

Shortly after the squad headed into the forest the relentless German Artillery began again and with it the familiar tree bursts. Orders were given immediately to dig in and wait out the barrage.

The Ninth Regiment's progress toward Aachen was slow as they continued to be bludgeoned by the unending enemy artillery and the need to dig in and wait it out.

As night fell on December 15th the German artillery fire ceased and the Second Squad remained in their holes, thankful for the silence. Sergeant Busi tried to rest in his hole but sleep was impossible. He had been on edge for so long that the war was now becoming unbearable and he felt as if he was breaking down. He was becoming obsessed with his own death and he now worried about it continuously. He had always accepted the fact that he would be killed, but the longer he remained alive the more he seemed to think about it. He had learned from men like Sergeant Hughes and other replacements that the men who feared death the most were usually the ones killed first. Still, it was impossible for him to stop thinking about his own mortality.

As he lay in his hole on December 15th he thought about how bad things were but he had no idea that the worst was yet to come.

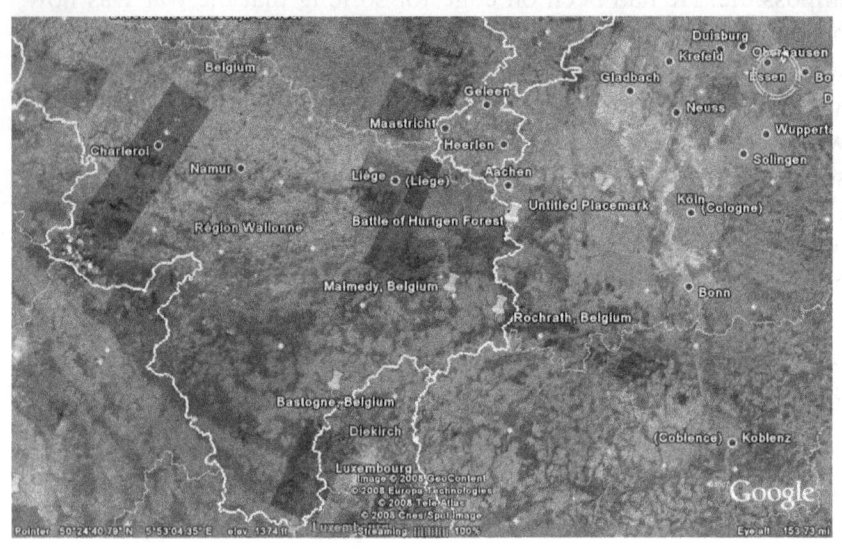

*Battle of Hurtgen Forest – December 1944 - center of map on German/Belgium border.
Bastogne and Luxembourg shown to far south.*

Map by Google Earth

Siegfried Line, left side of map from The Netherlands south to Switzerland.
Map by Google Images

Chapter 12

Death Awaits Them All
December 16th – 19th - The Battle of the Bulge
Lausdell Crossroads - Rocherath, Belgium

"We didn't know what was happening. I was so glad to get out of the forest I didn't care where they took me. All we knew was that the Germans had broken through our lines to our south and unless we moved out we would have been surrounded. What happened to us when we got to Rocherath was the worst fighting since D-Day. I thought it was the end for me. It was horrible."
Sergeant Joseph Busi interview 2005.

"Me and my friend Green were standing on a road in Stavelot (Belgium) and we looked across the river on the edge of town and the Krauts were coming over the hill toward us. They had so many tanks and infantry they looked like ants. They were screaming and running toward us so fast we didn't know what to do. We were on a two day pass and there were no officers, no orders just utter chaos. So we picked up our rifles and just fought. We couldn't stop tanks with our rifles so we just kept on retreating. It was December 17th and the Bulge had begun. It was frightening."
Sergeant Jack Derevensky (First Infantry Division) interview 2007.

After three straight days of constant shelling from the Nazi's in the Hurtgen Forest, Joe's nerves were frayed. The cold, snow and unending German artillery, left him feeling as if this was the end. For the first time since D-Day he knew deep in his heart that his end was near. He didn't know exactly how it would happen but he knew his demise was imminent. Maybe Eisenhower thought the Germans were beaten, but he could never have convinced the Sergeant that the war would be over by Christmas.

Hitler had been amassing some twenty-five divisions (over

two hundred thousand troops), ten of which were armored on a front that stretched eighty-five miles along the Belgium/Luxembourg German border, just east of the Siegfried Line. Their final offensive began on the morning of December 16th and the Second Division spread thinly along the northern shoulder of the Siegfried Line was getting ripped to shreds.

The Ninth Infantry was being cut off as the German spearhead broke through American lines just south of Busi's position in the Hurtgen Forest. The Nazis were no longer positioned just to the east of Second Division, but also to their south and dangerously close to splitting the Allied forces in two.

There was almost total chaos at the time the German offensive began, but the Second Division Commander, General Robertson acted quickly and decisively.

On the morning of December 16th orders were given to Sergeant Busi and rest of the Ninth Regiment to board trucks at their current positions in the Hurtgen Forrest.

Their destination, unknown to everyone but the top brass, was an area only about twenty-eight miles south of their current position. They were headed for the twin towns of Krinkelt and Rocherath that were just twenty miles north of the famous Belgian town of Bastogne.

The German plan for their spearhead, now known as the Battle of the Bulge, was to punch through the sparsely defended American Front and move all the way through Belgium to the port city of Antwerp. The Nazis would then have effectively cut the Allied Forces in two.

Hitler's last grasp at victory would come at a terrible price, both in Allied and German lives. The madman's orders were simple and direct. Break through the American lines and move to Antwerp at all costs. The German foot soldiers as well as officers were instructed not to take any prisoners. It would only bog down their advance and defeat was not an option. Complete and total annihilation of the Allies was the plan.

The Allies in December 1944 were convinced the war was almost over and Germany had been defeated. The surprise attack that began on December 16, 1944 took the American Forces by complete surprise and celebration was soon replaced by more death and destruction.

The Ninth Infantry Regiment was being positioned directly in the path of the German onslaught.

As the Sergeant boarded one of the trucks, he hoisted his thirty-caliber up on to the back of the truck and saw Colonel McKinley hustling up the muddy road toward him.

"Let's go, Let's go." The Colonel shouted as he waved his arms.

Busi sat down in the back of the truck next to Popielarcheck.

"Where we goin' Sarg?" Popielarcheck asked.

"I have no idea, but it's got to better than here." Busi responded.

The eight men of the Second Squad had no idea what fate awaited them. The trucks moved out and began the arduous journey south toward the twin towns of Krinkelt and Rocherath just inside the Belgium border. The distance was only twenty-eight miles but the trip took half a day. As they moved south along the half frozen, muddy roads, there were logjams of American convoys. Trucks, half-tracks and Jeeps lined the roads... some stuck in the mud, others just stopped, trying to negotiate the narrow Belgium roads. Chaos was the order of the day.

The Germans were attacking from the west and south and the thinly guarded American lines tried desperately to maintain control by shoring up weak spots in the front line. This meant moving men and equipment quickly. It was a daunting task.

The troop truck that transported Busi and his men ground to a halt on several occasions, bogged down in knee- deep mud. The dog-tired GIs had to unload and slop around the vehicle pushing the truck out of the quagmire time and time again. Exhausted with little food and no rest the Second Squad and rest of the Ninth moved slowly south toward their final destination.

Shortly after 3 P.M., the small convoy of trucks carrying the Second Squad and others moved south along a small dirt road a quarter mile east of the town of Rocherath.

The roads that crisscrossed the Belgium countryside were

mostly small dirt farm roads and extremely narrow. As Busi's truck continued he noticed two abandoned American vehicles on the right side of the road. One was a Jeep with a trailer still hitched and the other a half-track, obviously knocked out during a previous German artillery raid. He also noticed that the Jeep had a thirty-caliber heavy with loads of ammunition along with some mines and other rifles packed in the trailer that slid off the side of the road. The weapons were left in the trailer completely untouched, obviously abandoned by the hasty retreat of some unlucky GIs.

Just past the knocked out vehicles was a crossroad and just right of the crossroad was a rather large farmhouse with a huge barn both still in pristine condition. His truck continued another hundred yards to another dirt crossroad and stopped. This merging of several innocuous dirt roads was known as the Lausdell Crossroads and would become the scene of one of the most pivotal battles in the Battle of the Bulge.

"This is it boys." Lieutenant Tedman screamed.

Lieutenant Allyn Tedman had recently been put in charge of Company D and worked closely with Colonel McKinley.

Busi jumped from the truck, grabbed his thirty-caliber and laid it on the muddy road. The rest of the squad jumped from the back of the truck as the Lieutenant approached. Sergeant Roberts and the First Squad were in another truck that followed and they would set up side by side with Busi and the Second Squad.

"Sergeant set three guns up along this road and dig in!" the Lieutenant pointed east along the narrow dirt crossroad just a hundred yards from the farmhouse to his rear.

"Company B will be on your right flank two hundred yards and you are IT on the left flank. Your path of retreat is straight back to your left up that hill should you need it. You got that Sergeant?" The lieutenant barked.

"Yes Sir." Busi replied.

"What's goin' on Sir?" Busi came back.

"Not really sure, but the Krauts are busting through everywhere they can find a weak spot in our line. So hold your position here."

"Yes Sir." Busi responded.

Busi knew this could be bad. Very bad! The way the Germans were pounding them in the Hurtgen Forest, they were obviously planning a major attack and he just knew something was about to happen and it wasn't good.

The Lieutenant jumped back on the truck and headed west on the dirt road toward Rocherath.

"Popielarcheck, you and Peepsight get that number one gun down at the end of this road and dig in if you can." The Sergeant barked out the order.

Popielarcheck and Peepsight grabbed their thirty caliber and hustled down the road.

Busi turned to Sergeant Roberts.

"You want this corner Sergeant? I'll set my gun halfway down the road between you and Popeilarcheck. Busi asked Roberts.

"Yea, that will work…I need you on my flank in case things get ugly." Roberts replied.

Busi could see the concern on his men's faces as they moved into position along the road. They all knew something big was about to happen. The Sergeant noticed a huge artillery hole right at the corner of the crossroads. Roberts set his thirty caliber in the hole and Busi moved his gun about seventy-five yards to the east of Roberts. With the three heavy machine guns in place, all the approaches to the crossroad were covered and no one would be able to advance. At least that's what they thought.

The ground was almost completely frozen solid and Joe knew it would not be easy for any of the men to dig a foxhole for protection. This made things worse since the men manning the machine guns would be exposed to enemy fire with no protection. There was no alternative. The first two gun placements found it almost impossible to dig in. Their holes were crude and not very deep so they manned their guns lying on top of the cold snow almost completely exposed. Roberts' gun sat on top of the snow but at least he had an artillery hole for some protection.

As Joe helped finish setting up his gun he surveyed the surrounding landscape and made mental notes of what he saw.

It was near dusk and made it difficult for him to make out some of the features but he knew he might need this information later. The terrain was varied. As he looked to his left he saw the Krinkelt Forest about a quarter of mile. Large pine trees made a thick forest different from where he and his men were dug in. In front of him was a large field with a line of hedges that ran down the road on both sides. He surveyed his path of retreat behind him. There was another small field again lined with hedges four feet high on all four sides and another dirt road. The road cut through yet another larger field that gently sloped up to a hill lined at the top with a hedge. To his right was the crossroad to Rocherath and Company B about a quarter of mile. Behind and to his right was the farmhouse and barn. He noticed that there were very few trees, only hedges. There was snow. Lots of it…everywhere! Soldiers running uphill in retreat with Khaki colored uniforms made easy targets…especially during daylight hours.

Too many roads, and not much cover he thought. If things got bad their hasty retreat would be a slaughter with very few places to hide.

As darkness fell, it got cold…extremely cold. The temperature dropped below zero and the night of December 16th was the darkest and coldest night the Sergeant could remember. The next three nights would yield the same conditions. With no moon light Joe literally could not see his hand in front of his face. The Second squad waited and endured the cold and darkness. Several hours passed.

Sergeant Busi lay at his gun and listened. The silence was deafening. It was so quiet that an eerie feeling came over him. He began to shiver from the cold and his teeth rattled. Suddenly he heard someone walking on the road from behind. He didn't move or make a sound. It was so dark someone could pass him on the road and not even know he was there. The sound got closer and Busi moved the machine gun around toward the noise. It was Lieutenant Tedman who jumped in the hole next to the Sergeant and his Second gunner.

"Sergeant…seen anything?" the Lieutenant asked.

"No Sir! Nothing. What's goin' on?" Busi whispered.

"The Kraut have broken through our lines just southeast of here and the Ninety-Ninth Division has been almost completely wiped out. Right now we need to set up a defensive line so what's left of the Ninety-Ninth can get back here and regroup."

"How strong are the Krauts?" Busi asked.

"We don't exactly know, but it looks like a major offensive. Pass the word that the Ninety-Ninth is in retreat and they should be coming this way…don't be shooting them…they're banged up enough! Tedman replied.

"I'll pass the word."

Tedman disappeared into the night as he headed back to the Command Post set up in the farmhouse just to the rear.

The night passed slowly as the First and Second Squads manned their positions. All night long stragglers from the Ninety-Ninth Division continued to drift into the sector. Groups of only two or three GIs at a time stumbled back towards Busi and his men. They were disoriented, confused and almost none of the men had their weapons.

The Sergeant questioned a few of the poor souls who were retreating in chaos. He learned that the Germans were pouring everything they had into Honsfeld and Bullingen, two small Belgium towns just a few miles south and west of Rocherath.

What the Sergeant didn't know was that Hitler had sent his elite. *The First Panzer Division Leibstandarte Adolf Hitler and the 12th Panzer Division Hitler Jugend had been identified as the opposing force in early hours of the offensive. The 12th Panzer Division was the enemy force that opposed the British at Caen (France) earlier in the war and the Brits described the outfit as "filthy beasts…beyond fanatical!" They were elite troops, meticulously trained and personally sent to this sector by Hitler to assure success of the overall German strategy. Prior to the attack the division commander of the Hitler Jugend addressed his troops as follows:

"I ask of you, and expect of you, not to take any prisoners with the possible exception of some officers who might be kept alive for the purpose of questioning."

Their one aim was to kill, as brutally as possible.

What Hitler didn't know was that the Second Division had been re-deployed from the Hurtgen Forest to the Rocherath-

Elsenborn Area. Although the three infantry regiments making up the Second Division were spread thin along this area, Hitler and his commanders would soon find out that this group of hardened combat veterans was truly "second to none!" Although he had correctly estimated the strength and numbers of his opposition, he totally underestimated the tenacity, perseverance and toughness of the Second Division. The epic battle that was to ensue would be one of the great chapters in military history…and Sergeant Busi along with the heroic men of the Second Division would be right in the middle of it all.

As dawn approached on the 17th of December the troops from the Ninety-Ninth Division continued to pull back and were regrouping in the Elsenborn Ridge area some two miles west of Rocherath. The day dragged on as Busi and his men sat in their positions frozen by the frigid Belgium winter.

There was little food and the Allies were in such disarray that it was impossible for any supplies to reach the makeshift front line. Hungry, exhausted and totally on edge for several days now the men continued to struggle just to survive the weather and lack of nourishment. Their feet were frozen and many of the men who were not killed would suffer permanent damage to fingers and toes. The conditions were miserable, but the troops persevered with no complaints. As the day passed more and more information was gathered from the ragged Ninety-Ninth Division as they continued to stagger back in retreat. Word had spread that the Krauts were shooting prisoners and surrender was not an option for the Americans.

By late afternoon rumors began floating between Busi and his troops. There were unconfirmed reports that there had been a horrific massacre outside the town of Malmedy, just twenty miles south west of Rocherath. One hundred- twenty American prisoners were gathered in a field outside the town and killed as the Nazis machined gunned all of the unarmed soldiers. When the machine guns stopped the SS Troops walked among the dead and any American that showed any signs of life was shot through the head with small arms fire.

When the men of the First and Second Squads heard the

terrible news that would come to be known as the "Malmedy Massacre" they became enraged and their resolve even more meaningful.

Hours passed and the cold dark night of December 17th fell on the unfortunate GIs of the Second Division. Busi was moving up and down the road making sure his men and the men of the First Squad were still coherent and encouraged them to hang on.

At about 1900 hours (7:00 P.M.) Busi was huddled at the corner artillery hole with Roberts and his First Gunner. The men discussed their situation and commented on the deafening silence.

Just then the silence was broken. The unmistakable clanking sounds of German Panther Tanks broke the night silence. Approaching Busi's position head on, from the south, was the first of what would be many German Tanks that would try to make their way to Rocherath.

"Tanks?" Busi questioned Roberts in a loud whisper.

"Yea, great." Roberts replied.

"We've got three thirty calibers, a dozen rifle grenades and some mines…what's going on?" Busi pressed knowing that he could not defend against tanks.

"I don't know Sergeant but I guess we'll find out." Roberts replied

Roberts was not very reassuring.

The Panthers slowly clanked closer and closer and as they approached the crossroads the Sergeant heard voices speaking in German rather loudly as if the Krauts were coming down Main St. marching in a parade. It was so dark none of the three men in the artillery hole could see anything. And they assumed that the opposite was true.

Busi and Roberts decided to crawl along the side of the road that went directly behind them toward the farmhouse. Between the road and the two GIs was a three- foot high hedge with no leaves so it was possible for the men to see what was on the road…if they could see anything. As the two crawled on their bellies along the hedge the first Panther Tank roared past the crossroad, and continued to the next intersection.

The two men lay perfectly still as the huge monster clanked

passed them... not more than six feet away! Busi turned on his back and caught sight of the Panther as he looked up into the night sky that was just slightly lighter than the darkness at ground level. He watched as the death machine went by and then saw German Soldiers walking behind the tank...so close to him he could literally reach his hand out and grab one by a boot. They were yakking like little schoolgirls as they passed. Busi counted about thirty. The small force continued up the road and turned left past the Farmhouse at the next crossroad and headed toward Rocherath. The German contingent had no idea that the Ninth Regimental headquarters was located in the Farmhouse not twenty-five feet from the road they were on.

"What the hell is goin' on? Are they giving up?" Busi whispered to Roberts.

"I don't know but by the looks of that Panther, I'd say no!" Roberts didn't have any answers.

Not more than three minutes passed and another Panther approached from the same road and Busi could now hear more than just one. The answer to the Sergeant's question was now obvious.

"Sounds like the whole fucking German Army is coming down that road." Roberts whispered as the next monster approached the crossroad.

The two Sergeants did not move an inch. Again the tank passed by with soldiers in tow, walking like they were out for a stroll in the park. Busi looked up again at the night sky and counted the number of Germans...at least thirty that he could see. Their chatter was obvious and disconcerting. Dozens of thoughts raced through his head. Did they know where they were...that there could possibly be Americans six feet away? They seemed so sure of themselves as if the war was over and they were marching to victory! Was he and the entire company now behind enemy lines?

The tank and soldiers continued on the same route, turning left in front of the farmhouse in the direction of Rocherath. Within a matter of a minute a third Panther approached again. Same routine. The two Americans lying in the cold snow watched in horror as the third Panther passed with another platoon behind. This group turned left at the first crossroad where Roberts' gun was set up. They too were headed for Rocherath. As the third tank passed there was a break. Busi and Roberts stood up and scurried back to the artillery hole and the thirty-caliber.

Roberts' First Gunner was hidden in the hole with the thirty caliber. It was so dark the Germans walked right past and never saw the heavy sitting on its tripod at the corner of the crossroad.

"What the hell is goin' on?" the private asked.

Busi ignored the Private.

"We've got to do something! We have some mines. Let's lay some on the road they're comin' in on and see if we can knock out a few. At least we would have a chance to stop them." Busi suggested to Roberts.

"Grab two each! You too private…let's go we have to move." Roberts barked.

The three men grabbed the mines that were lying at the bottom of the artillery hole and ran across the intersection. They laid down six anti-tank mines in a random pattern on the sides of the road where the tracks of the Panthers would surely pass. The anti-tank mines would not be able to completely destroy the huge Panther Tank but it would cause enough damage to disable it or possibly set it ablaze. It was their only hope.

After they laid the deadly traps the three ran back to their hole and the Private got behind the thirty-caliber. Within minutes Busi heard all hell breaking loose in the direction of Rocherath. The three tanks and ninety plus German infantrymen had obviously come to the end of their parade. The unsuspecting Nazis ran right in the middle of the rest of the Ninth Regiment including Companies A and B positioned on the northeast perimeter of Rocherath. The sounds of the screaming wounded and explosions caused by the mighty Panther Tanks could be heard by Busi and his men a half-mile away.

It was now 2030 hours (8:30P.M.). The Second squad sat and waited and listened…but not for long. Within a few minutes the stark reality of their situation continued. A fourth Panther was heard moving toward the crossroads.

The Sergeant knew that the German Army approaching his position would have to be stopped at some point. If they were allowed to continue to advance they would overwhelm the rest of the Regiment and he and his men would be killed or captured. It was an impossible feat since they were not prepared to stop tanks. They just didn't have the necessary weapons. Unless there was the unlikely appearance of a just a few American Sherman Tanks to counter this offensive, he knew this would be his demise.

He peered over the mound of the hole and stared into the darkness, unable to see yet another approaching Panther. It roared closer until it rolled to an area of the road where the anti-tank mines were laid. Nothing. The monster continued toward his position. Still nothing. The Panther reached the crossroad and began to turn left. Suddenly it happened. The Panther hit the last of the mines with its right track and there was a horrific explosion. Busi and his hole mates ducked as debris flew from the explosion.

The tank continued to turn onto the crossroad for another fifteen feet and ground to a halt. The right track had been completely blown apart and the huge monster came to rest just as it had made the turn, totally disabled blocking the road to Rocherath. The platoon of German Soldiers following the tank broke ranks and sprinted back down the road disappearing into the night.

The engine continued to idle as the turret with its huge seventy-five millimeter gun traversed the countryside. It moved right and all the way around three hundred-sixty degrees as if the men inside were looking for something to shoot at. Suddenly a blast from the monster gun shattered the night. Busi and his hole mates ducked as the ground shook from the blast. The turret moved another ninety degrees and let loose another blast that again shattered the night silence. The Nazis inside were firing indiscriminately to scare the hell out of anyone who dared get close to the disabled tank. Again the turret moved and again another giant blast.

The third time was the charm as the huge seventy-five millimeter shell struck the barn next to the farm house one hundred yards away. The barn exploded in flames like kindling and a huge fireball erupted. The barn began to burn profusely with flames reaching thirty to forty feet high. The blaze lit up the pitch-black Belgium night like it was midday. Now, everything in the immediate area was clearly visible. Busi and Roberts watched as the monster turret continued to traverse and fire indiscriminately several more times shaking the very ground they were on.

"We've got to do something." Busi blurted out.

"We've got some rifle grenades, but I don't think they'll do much against that armor." Roberts replied.

Busi reached down below his feet where the mines and rifle grenades were lying and picked up the long narrow stick-like weapon with a pineapple looking grenade attached to the end. He stuck the stick down the barrel of his M-1 and inserted a blank cartridge. He peered over the top of the bunker and aimed the rifle at the huge monster tank and fired. The grenade hit the heavy armor of the tank just above the disabled track and bounced off on to the ground and exploded.

The explosion did nothing to the tank but the occupants now rotated the turret in the direction of the sound of the grenade hitting the tank and fired off a round. The huge shell screamed over Busi's head and exploded fifty yards behind him. The tank was too close to Busi and Roberts and the gun could not move any lower…it was impossible for the giant gun to blow Busi and his hole mates to bits. Busi realized this and grabbed another rifle grenade and repeated his actions…this time the grenade landed directly under the barrel, in a small opening between the gun turret and the hull. The grenade lodged in the opening and exploded. A huge flame billowed from under the big gun and Busi could hear the moan of the motor as the Nazis inside tried in vane to traverse the turret to another position. The grenade's explosion now froze the turret and the massive Panther Tank was completely immobilized. Although it could not move, the Panther was still a threat and needed to be destroyed.

The quick thinking Busi remembered the abandoned jeep and half-track toward his rear.

"Private, get Popielarcheck and get back to that abandoned Jeep along the road we came in on. There were two gas cans on the back of the Jeep. Bring them back here on the double….and stay low!" He instructed Roberts' First Gunner.

"Ok Sarg." the private replied…and he was gone.

"What'd you have in mind, Joe?" Roberts asked.

"We can't blow them up but we can burn the Nazi bastards right in their own tank." Busi replied.

"Great idea…I just hope those gas cans have gas in them." Roberts said hopefully.

The tank sat quietly as if the occupants were deciding what to do next. Sounds of machine gun fire and blasts from Rocherath a half-mile away indicated that the first three tanks were still engaging the rest of the Ninth Regiment.

Within a few minutes the Private and Popielarcheck returned with two cans of gasoline full to the top. They jumped into the artillery hole where Busi and Roberts were waiting and dropped the cans at the bottom of the hole.

"You two, man this gun. We're gonna' burn those bastards out of there. Fix this gun on that hatch and if you see so much as a crack in that hatch, open up and blast the shit out of them! Got it?" Busi commanded.

"Yes, Sarge." Popielarcheck replied as he jumped behind the thirty caliber.

Roberts grabbed one heavy five-gallon gas can and the two Sergeants climbed out of their hole. They moved up behind the disabled Panther clearly visible from the light of the burning barn. Roberts removed the cap and tried to lift the can up by himself but it was too heavy. Busi grabbed one end and helped Roberts lift the can on to the back of the hull of the tank. Once the can was on the hull they dumped the can over and the gas began to gurgle out all over the back of the hull. As the gas continued to spill out, Busi noticed the hatch on top of the turret open slightly.

"Brrrrrrrp!"

A blast from Popielarcheck's gun blasted the hatch as the bullets hit the armor and sparked as they bounced off. The hatch immediately slammed shut but not before the Nazis inside threw an object out of the hatch and on to the hull, three feet away from the two Sergeants now crouched low. It was a phosphorous grenade. The Germans tossed it out to scare the GIs who might be trying to enter the tank.

The grenade exploded and the blast immediately ignited the gas… there was a tremendous explosion. The blast threw the two

GIs to the ground as the flames roared up on the hull of the tank.

"*Oh shit...I'm hit!*" Roberts screamed out as he grabbed his left hand with his right.

Busi grabbed Roberts' hand as the two lay side by side on the frozen dirt road. He saw a hole that was now bleeding profusely and the two Sergeants ran quickly back to their hole. Busi grabbed a dirty rag from his pocket and wrapped Roberts' hand with it. The burning tank lit up the darkness enough for Joe to see the wound in Roberts' hand. Shrapnel from the German grenade blew a hole right through Roberts' hand and he needed medical attention.

"Get back to the farm house...there has to be a medic around there somewhere...go,go,go." Busi shouted at Roberts.

Roberts headed back to the farmhouse. Busi never saw Roberts again.

The tank continued to burn and the occupants tried several times to escape the inferno only to be blasted by the thirty-caliber machine gun locked on their position. The hatch opened slightly and closed quickly as Popielarcheck's gun blasts drove the burning occupants back into their fiery coffin. The Sergeant thought how ironic it was that the tide had turned on the Germans after the hedgerow incident some five months earlier when his buddies lay dying in their Sherman Tank as it burned.

Unfortunately for the German pair burning alive in their steel coffin, there would be no hero to rescue them from their fate. They became desperate and no longer able to tolerate the immense heat mounting inside, threw the hatch open. One of the Germans tried to quickly jump from the turret.

"Brrrrrrrp!" A blast from Popielarcheck sprayed the Nazi as he tried to climb out of the turret. He was hit immediately and fell down the side of the tank and on to the dirt road, motionless. Suddenly, without warning, the other tank occupant leapt from the turret so quickly Popielarcheck's gun missed him as he jumped down on the hull and on to the dirt road. As soon as he hit the ground he ran like a deer back down the same road he had come in on just a few hours earlier. He had a white bandana or bandage wrapped around his head that was illuminated by the lights of the burning tank as he streaked across the open meadow.

First and Second Squad machine guns roared as the Nazi tried to evade the onslaught of the Americans. Busi pulled his rifle up and also joined in the target practice. The Nazi continued to run so fast that he may have made it to safety, as he seemed to disappear into the darkness.

The immediate conflict at the Lausdell Crossroads was over. The Panther Tank and the ill-fated barn continued to burn. The First and Second Squads had prevailed with Sergeant Roberts as the one minor casualty. The two squads waited, anticipating more action, but all was quiet for now. The Krauts had halted their attack for now, not knowing the real strength of the force that lie in front of them.

Joe lay back in his hole at the corner of Main St. and Hell. He heard tank and small arms fire coming from the town of Rocherath, no doubt from the three previous Panthers that had past hours earlier.

Lieutenant Tedman made a visit to Busi's hole a few hours later. The sounds of battle had subsided and Tedman informed the Sergeant that the rest of the Ninth Regiment located in Rocherath had destroyed the three Panther Tanks with no more than just a few bazookas and an anti-tank gun. The German infantrymen that past right in front of Busi's Squad had been wiped out but the American losses were also quite heavy.

Busi asked the Lieutenant if he could expect any support in the way of Sherman Tanks. Tedman promised nothing and told him what he had now was it and no further troops or tank support was coming. The Second I.D. was spread thin along the "Northern Shoulder" of the battle and he and his men were to hold their positions until given further orders. The Lieutenant returned to Headquarters located in the farmhouse about one hundred yards to the rear of the Crossroads.

Since Roberts was wounded and out of action, Busi was now in charge of both squads. Throughout the night he made his way from hole to hole making sure his men understood what was happening. He finally settled in his small hole at the corner of the crossroads sometime around 0300 hours (3 A.M.). He could hear the sounds of tanks maneuvering far off in the Krinkelt Forest to his south and east throughout the night.

Bitter cold and the total darkness continued for yet another night. The huge barn and destroyed Panther Tank that burned so brightly were now just smoldering heaps, victims of the savagery that took place earlier. Sleep was impossible and Sergeant Busi pondered his fate. He knew the Germans were assessing the situation and probably thought it best to wait until daylight to determine the true strength of their enemy. He also knew that he and his men could not turn away Panther Tanks with machine guns and unless American Shermans were headed his way to meet the German onslaught, they would all be killed. But as the good soldier he was, he accepted his fate, whatever it was. He would fight the enemy until he could no longer do so and if it meant death, then so be it…it was out of his control.

The bitter cold began to take its toll. It became difficult for the Sergeant to feel his feet as the temperature began to drop below zero. His thoughts now turned to freezing to death as his teeth chattered from the cold…but he continued to endure the suffering.

The cold Belgium night dragged on but at least it was quiet for now. After the battle sounds from the town ceased it became eerily quiet. Only the far away sounds from the forest of the constant maneuvering of enemy tanks could be heard. It was disconcerting for the Sergeant to think about how strong the enemy was just a few hundred yards from his position.

As daybreak approached on December 18th the noise level of tanks deep in the Krinkelt Forest became more noticeable.

It seemed as if the entire forest was crawling with heavy machinery and Busi realized that the Germans were again on the move. Unlike the night before when the Panthers lumbered right down Main Street, the noises now seemed to come from everywhere…everywhere to his east.

Shortly after daybreak it all began. The morning was very misty as the German Army moved on the entire American Front.

Through the haze Busi could see Panther Tanks moving out of the Krinkelt Forest into the open fields directly in front of his position a half-mile away. This time instead of a line of tanks crawling down the small Belgium roads, the Panthers were side by side with hundreds of troops behind the behemoths. As the giant tanks and rest of the German Army rolled over the snowy fields, Busi prepared for the onslaught. He huddled over his thirty caliber with his First gunner PFC Hooper a recent replacement Busi hardly knew.

"Holy shit Sarg, it looks like the whole damn German Army is coming." Hooper exclaimed.

"God Damn it...get out all the ammo we got." Busi ordered.

"How we gonna stop 'em Sarg?" Hooper asked.

"I don't know." Busi replied with his eyes fixed on the approaching force.

Just then the seventy-five millimeter guns of the Panthers began to unload. Busi counted at least twelve tanks with hundreds of troops in support. It was an unbelievable sight. Shells began exploding everywhere as the massive guns unleashed their fury on the near defenseless platoon.

Luckily the command post located directly behind the platoon's position had an artillery spotter attached and began calling in coordinates to the Second Division Artillery located several miles to the rear of the Ninth Regiment. The Second Division Artillery began laying a barrage of artillery fire right in the middle of the German attack force. The noise was deafening as both sides threw every thing they had at each other...and in the middle was the Ninth Regiment. Busi and his men watched as the German hoard continued toward their position but at a great cost. As the American Artillery zeroed in on the Germans, bodies flew in the air and several tanks were hit immediately, exploding into flames. Some were obliterated into flying debris that killed many more German troops.

Busi's men tried desperately to cover from the seventy-five millimeter explosions, now getting closer. Although the artillery was a godsend, the German advance continued as many more Panthers and hundreds of troops continued to pour out of the forest and head toward Busi and his men. It was a horrific sight and Busi knew this was the end. As the German Troops got within machine gun range, the First and Second Squads opened fire. The artillery continued to rain down on the Germans, but they continued to advance. There was no way to stop them. Hundreds of Nazis were machine gunned to death as they approached the Lausdell Crossroads but they continued to advance. Several Panthers were now within two hundred yards of the doomed American Platoon. Busi could see Company B to his west taking a pounding from many tanks that had begun to overrun their position.

Busi looked to his right flank and noticed that all three machine gun positions from Company B had been destroyed and all the GIs were dead. He knew it would not be long before he and his men would be overrun as well.

At that moment, Lieutenant Tedman ran through the maze of explosions and jumped in Busi's hole.

"*Get your men out of here, now!*" Tedman screamed through the noise of the battle.

Busi reacted immediately.

"*Retreat, Retreat*!! He screamed and gave the arm signal to do the same.

Both squads saw the signal and began to retreat. Their path of retreat was straight back, across the road and to an exposed field that went slightly uphill. That field would be the death of many of them simply because of the lack of cover. As the men retreated Busi saw several men cut down as they tried to make their way back. It was horrible to watch.

"*Go Sergeant, I'll stay at this gun while you move back.*" Tedman shouted.

Busi could see that the Lieutenant had a head wound and was bleeding down the left side of his face.

"*No Lieutenant, you go…you're wounded, I'll stay.*" Busi screamed back through the deafening sounds of gunfire and explosions.

Tedman didn't argue and Busi watched as the Lieutenant made his way back. As The Sergeant looked to make sure all of his men had begun the retreat, he looked to his left where Popielarcheck and Peepsight had their thirty-caliber set up. Popielarcheck was gone but Peepsight was still there firing his gun. Busi screamed and waved his arms at Peepsight to retreat, but

Peepsight continued to fire.

Busi had stopped firing his gun so he would not give away his position. He removed the firing pin to disable the gun and waited for the right moment as he planned his escape. He could now see as many as twenty Panther Tanks scattered throughout the fields leading to his position. The German Soldiers numbered in the hundreds. The American artillery continued to rain down on the massive invaders but they continued to advance.

As he grabbed the pin he looked at Peepsight one more time. At that moment a Panther had zeroed in on Peepsight's position and fired a round right into him. The explosion blew Peepsight twenty feet straight up into the air as his body parts flew in all directions, along with the thirty- caliber. Busi watched in horror as his long time friend was blown to pieces. Peepsight was gone. He had been with the squad since D-Day +1 and it was all over for him now. Busi didn't have time to ponder his friend's fate. He realized that it was his turn to retreat, as the massive German attack got closer. He knew his chances of surviving this retreat were slim. He stood up out of his small hole and threw the firing pin from his gun toward the advancing Germans. He was out of his mind with rage and anger.

"Stick this up your ass, you fuckin' Nazi bastards. he screamed at the top of his lungs as he threw the pin at his enemy.

The Sergeant turned and sprinted toward the road winding his way back as bullets whizzed past him. Several seventy-five millimeter shells exploded within yards of him as he moved, miraculously missing him. He was completely exposed now as he tried to find cover. He reached the next road and hurdled the barbed wire fence that ran the length of the road. He landed on the other side of the fence and threw himself into a ditch that had a small amount of icy running water.

More bullets flew over his head and several more explosions went off just past where he landed in the ditch. The Germans knew he was there and they kept advancing. He lay face down in the ditch totally out of breath, with the side of his face immersed in the small trickle of ice-cold water. He waited for another thirty seconds and jumped to his feet. He now had to sprint up the small hill with no cover and he knew he would be lucky to make it. In a serpentine motion he ran as fast as he had ever run in his life. Sprays of bullets flew past his head, some hitting the ground and snow on all sides. Several more shells hit close as the German tanks tried to zero in on the lone GI.

Amazingly, he could see the top of the hill now with the four foot hedgerow just yards away. If he could just make it to the hedgerow! He continued up the hill, unscathed to the hedgerow. He hurdled the hedgerow like an Olympian and dove to safety on the backside…he was totally exhausted. Not ten yards away to his left was Popielarcheck and an unknown private from Company B crouched behind the hedgerow. As Busi caught his breath he peeked over the top of the hedgerow to see the Germans had overrun their original machine gun positions at the Crossroads and were continuing on toward the farmhouse and burned out barn.

"We've got to get out of here." Busi told Pop.

"I know Sarg…but we need to be careful. Those bastards are right down the hill." Pop responded.

Just then hovering close to the ground and approaching from the rear, out of nowhere, came Colonel McKinley. He ran up to the three men and started barking orders.

"You men need to hold this hill at all costs…understood?" McKinley demanded.

"Yes Sir." Busi replied.

"There's a machine gun in that abandoned half-track down that road. Get it, set up and hold this hill…we must hold this hill!" McKinley barked out, turned and ran back as quickly as he came.

"Shit, doesn't look like we're going anywhere boys." Busi announced to his fellow stranded GIs.

McKinley's order to "hold at all costs," meant that they were to stay in their positions and hold off the enemy until the enemy either retreated or killed them all! There would be no enemy retreat in this battle. Busi and his ill-fated buddies knew that this was a suicide order. They knew they would be over run and killed, but as good soldiers they followed their Colonel's orders.

"Let's go get that gun…we have to hurry." Busi continued.

Popielarcheck and the Private followed Busi to the

abandoned half-track just a few yards down the same dirt road that led them to this mess just a few days earlier. The Private picked up the gun, Popielarcheck picked up the tripod and Busi grabbed two cans of ammo. The three started back up the hill to the hedgerow. The hedgerow was perpendicular to the road so it gave good cover from the advancing Germans. The three stopped at the junction of the road and the hedgerow.

"O.K. Private take the gun to the other side of this hedgerow. We'll set it up over there…and stay low." Busi ordered.

"Yes, Sarg."

The Private stayed low and ran to the opposite end of the hedgerow about seventy-five yards away.

"Pop get over there with that tripod and I'll be right behind you…*and stay low behind that hedge.*" The Sergeant again ordered.

Popielarcheck put the tripod over his shoulders and began running along the hedge, bent almost in half so as not to seen by the advancing Germans. Busi followed about twenty yards behind with the ammo. As Popielarcheck got about half way to his destination he began to straighten his body upward. His upper torso was now above the four-foot hedgerow and completely exposed. Busi saw the paratrooper begin to expose himself and heard the Germans at the bottom of the hill begin shouting. They had spotted Popielarcheck!

"Pop get down, get down, get down! Busi screamed at Popielarcheck.

The paratrooper didn't hear Busi's screams through the sounds of the battle and continued to unconsciously stand up, now almost completely upright, as he ran along the back of the hedge.

Busi dropped his ammo boxes and sprinted toward Popielarcheck. The Sergeant thought that if he could get to him in time he could knock the paratrooper down and save his life. The Sergeant got to within three feet of Popielarcheck when a seventy-five millimeter shell came screaming across the hill, over the hedgerow and hit Popielarcheck right in the upper half of his body. The shell exploded and blew Busi in the air ten feet back. The Sergeant lay on his back behind the hedge unconscious.

When the Sergeant regained his consciousness he tried to

remember what had happened. His vision began to come back to him as he opened his eyes and was looking straight up at the sky. He was totally deaf from the concussion of the shell. His head throbbed with a terrible headache and his whole body felt as if it were on fire. The pain throughout his body was intense. As he rolled over on his left side his memory began to come back to him. The War, Belgium, retreat, Popielarcheck…all these thoughts now raced through his aching head. Then he saw a sight that shocked him. A pair of human legs lay ten feet away from him in perfect form as if someone had sheered off a human body at the waist and placed them on the ground. They were Popierlarchek's legs still in his paratrooper pants and his combat boots still on his feet. The tripod he had over his shoulders and the entire upper half of his body were gone.

    The Sergeant tried to gather himself, but any movement was extremely difficult. He had blood dripping from his nose and his helmet was gone. As he looked at his own torso he saw that he was covered in blood and pieces of human tissue, none larger than a quarter…he was covered with what was left of Pvt. Popielarcheck's upper body.

    His right hand had a large hole in the soft tissue between his thumb and forefinger and the pain was excruciating. The blood oozed from the wound. His right leg throbbed with horrible pain and as he tried to sit up he became light headed and began to pass out again. He quickly laid his head back down on the ground and closed his eyes. He had a terrible ringing in his ears that was deafening.

    He felt the need to puke so he again rolled over on his left side and expelled the miniscule contents of his stomach. He opened his eyes again only to witness what was left of his paratrooper friend. He looked down the length of the hedgerow and the private carrying the machine gun had either been blown to pieces or decided to retreat. The only weapon he saw was his forty-five-caliber sidearm that was still strapped to his belt. For the first time since D-Day he felt completely hopeless.

    Sergeant Busi knew this was his end. For six months he wondered how and when it would happen and now his answer was clear. His life would end right here on a miserable, cold Belgium morning in a desolate frozen battlefield, thousands of miles from his Pennsylvania home.

As he lay there in complete agony he promised himself he would not give up on his life until his enemy shot him dead. He was still barely alive, but his fierce determination and toughness forced him to continue on.

He had to move…he had to get somewhere to the rear. Then he realized that he had no idea how long he had been unconscious. Had the Germans passed over him believing he was dead? If that were the case, he was now behind enemy lines and if discovered in his condition he would be shot for sure. These thoughts raced through his head as he struggled to gain his composure.

Now the sounds of war returned as his hearing began to come back and he focused on his surroundings. Artillery shells exploded down the hill and he crawled back to the hedge to get a peek.

As he peered over the hedge he saw the Germans were still at the bottom of the hill. The American artillery was impeding the German advance just enough to allow the Sergeant time to move. He knew that he was only unconscious for a few seconds.

He had pain in every part of his body as he tried to stumble to his feet. He collapsed in a heap as he tried to stand on his right leg. He looked at his right leg and saw blood coming from a hole on the inside of his lower calf about six inches above his ankle. Shrapnel from the seventy-five had ripped a hole in his muscle rendering his leg useless. His only option now was to crawl. As he looked down the length of the hedge he saw the Krinkelt Forest about two hundred yards away with its dense pine trees. Although this route was parallel to the German lines it was his only hope for cover. If he tried to crawl straight back through the open fields, he would surely be spotted and shot.

And so he began to crawl on his belly, over the frozen field along the hedge, dragging his useless leg and enduring unbearable pain. Blood continued to pour from his nose and into his mouth. The concussion of the seventy-five millimeter blast was so strong that it was as if someone had hit him in the face with a baseball bat.

It broke the blood vessels in his nose and created a blood clot in the front part of his brain. He had shrapnel in his right hand and right leg, but continued to crawl over icy snow and mud toward safety.

As he crawled along the hedgerow, bodies and body parts were strewn everywhere. Many men from his platoon were blown to bits as they retreated, trying to make it to the safety of the forest. There was no one alive and he felt terribly alone. What happened to the rest of the Ninth Infantry? Were they all dead? Where was everyone?

He continued to crawl on his belly. He was covered with mud and his hands were frozen from the snow. He tried again to stand but it was impossible. The pain throughout his body was unbearable but he kept on. American artillery continued to pound the German positions and kept them at bay at least for a short time. As he crawled to the edge of forest he stopped and laid his head on the cold snowy ground. Blood from his nose spilled out onto the white snow coloring it a rich red color. He realized he was dying and prayed to his Savior for strength.

The snow was cold on his face but eased his headache a bit. He was completely exhausted, but he had made it to the cover of the thick forest.

Suddenly he heard a voice. An American voice.

"Hey! Soldier…soldier…come on…keep coming. He heard a voice call out to him in a loud whisper from inside the tree line.

Busi picked up his head and looked in the direction of the voice. His vision was somewhat blurry but he could make out two figures crouched in a bunker just inside the tree line. One figure was waving at him to keep coming.

Busi gathered the strength and began crawling toward the figures. They spoke English but that was no guarantee that they were American Soldiers. As he crawled closer he could see both men had American helmets and one soldier had a pair of binoculars around his neck. He crawled up to the side of the bunker and the two men grabbed him by the back of his torn jacket and dragged him into a rather large crater. He collapsed at the bottom of the bunker and one of the men rolled him over on his back. As Busi looked at the American Soldiers he saw a red cross on the helmet of one of the men. He was a medic! The other soldier was an artillery spotter for the Second Division Artillery and was transmitting enemy coordinates to the artillery at the rear. Busi had a sense of relief as the medic began to work on him.

"Where you hit soldier?" the medic questioned as he tried to figure out where all the blood and human tissue had come from.

"My right hand and my right leg, I think….and my head feels bad." The Sergeant responded in a daze as he raised his right hand for the medic.

"Anywhere else?"

"I don't really know…my body is burning all over." Busi continued.

The medic grabbed Busi's hand, poured some sulfur powder over the small hole and wrapped it with a clean white bandage from his medic pack. The medic then worked his way down the Sergeant's right leg to find the shrapnel wound that tore open a huge hole in his calf muscle. He grabbed a clean cloth from his bag and began cleaning out the wound. He again covered the hole with sulfur powder and wrapped the wounded leg with a fresh gauze bandage.

"Who are you and what outfit are you with?" the medic asked.

"Sergeant Busi, Company D, Ninth Infantry…do you have any water?" he responded.

The medic handed Busi a full canteen of water. The Sergeant guzzled almost half of the contents.

"The Ninth is really takin' a beating in Rocherath, but they're tough as hell…What's all this meat all over you?" the medic asked as he began picking pieces of the red tissue off Busi's neck and shoulders.

"It's what's left of a Private that was hit by a shell, right in front of me." Busi replied.

"Sorry about that Sergeant." the medic's voice lowered as he continued to clean up his patient.

The artillery spotter continued to communicate coordinates over his radio to the rear as the American shells flew overhead.

The medic grabbed yet another gauze and began wiping

Busi's face, especially under his nose that continued to drain thick red blood. He pushed two small cotton balls up each of his nostrils to try to stop the bleeding. He pulled down on Busi's lower left eyelid and checked his pupils.

"Get hit in the head, Sergeant?" he asked.

"Not that I know of…a shell went off a few yards away and it felt like someone hit me in the face with a club…I passed out." Busi responded.

"You're lucky, Sergeant…if the shrapnel didn't kill you the concussion from the explosion sure should have. You need to get back to the rear Sergeant. The doctors need to look at you. I have to stay here so you're on your own. Besides, the way the Krauts are moving we're gonna' have to pull back. Just go straight back. Can you walk?" The medic asked.

"I don't think so…I don't know."

"Well, you can't stay here, so do the best you can…you better get moving… the Krauts are close." the medic ordered.

The Sergeant felt a little stronger with some rest and help from the medic. He climbed to his feet, stood on his left leg and began to limp out of the bunker putting as little pressure as possible on his wounded leg.

The battle continued around him as he made his way to the rear. He slowly limped along the tree line and used the forest as cover but was limited in his movements. He could only limp twenty or thirty yards at a time before the pain in his wounded leg became unbearable and he was forced to lie down in the snow.

He felt light headed and dizzy as the pain in his head throbbed continuously. Blood continued to drain from his nose and the two cotton balls the medic had shoved up his nostrils were gone. The blood flowed down his lip and into his mouth. He tried stop the blood flow with is torn sleeves but to no avail. When he stopped to rest he spat out the blood that drained into his mouth and it seemed to be getting worse. The bandages the medic had applied to his shrapnel wounds in his leg and hand were now soaked through with his blood. He looked at his right hand and it was now so swollen that it was impossible for him to move any of his fingers.

After several stops he came upon another artillery bunker and as he approached he could hear the cries for help from a wounded soldier. He fell into the bunker and rolled over next to a GI whose right leg was broken at the knee so badly that it was bent at a ninety-degree angle away from the midline of his body. The GI moaned in agony and pleaded for The Sergeant to help him. Busi could barely help himself but he crawled over to the ill-fated GI and tried to pull down on the leg that was snapped at an angle. The wounded soldier shrieked in agony as Busi tried to straighten the leg. He stopped immediately. He was unable to move the shattered limb and was only causing the soldier pure agony.

"I can't help you soldier. I'm moving back. As soon as I see a medic I'll send him to get you, O.K? Hang on someone will come for you, I promise." he said as he realized he made a promise he may not be able to keep.

Busi tried to comfort the GI and felt dreadful for having to leave a fellow soldier in agony. The Sergeant rested for a minute or so and dragged himself out of the bunker as the wounded soldier pleaded with him to stay and help. As difficult as it was, he ignored the pleading GI and continued his journey, barely able to walk himself.

He had lost a lot of blood and the persistent bleeding from his wounds began to take its toll as he became weaker and weaker. Hundreds of mangled bodies littered the ground as he moved among the trees to what he hoped would be safety. The Ninety-Ninth and Second Divisions had taken many casualties as they retreated and tried to regroup toward the rear. The German attack was relentless.

He had been moving for almost an hour and covered only about three quarters of a mile to the rear. He was totally exhausted and extremely weak from the loss of blood. He made one final stretch to a small clearing in the forest and saw huge artillery crater. He dragged himself closer to it and decided that this may be as far as he could go. He was light headed and felt as if he would pass out. As he approached the huge hole in the ground he couldn't believe his eyes. Sitting at the bottom of the hole were eight American GIs in various degrees of incapacitation. Several were already dead and the remaining four or five were severely wounded.

Busi jumped into the hole with his fallen soldiers and decided that this was end of his journey…he could no longer go on. He lay down next to one of the Americans and looked at his battered body. The GI had most of his left arm blown off and his head had terrible lacerations. As he looked around most of the others were in a similar condition.

"What outfit are you guys with?" Busi asked.

A soldier sitting across from Busi responded.

"Most of us are with the Ninety-Ninth but those two were with the Second ." He pointed to two of the mutilated bodies lying face down about five feet in front of him.

"What about you?" he asked the Sergeant.

"Second." Busi responded.

"We really took a pounding the last few days…we tried to get to Elsenborn to regroup, but this is as far as we could go." The soldier added.

"Well boys, I just came from Rocherath and the Krauts are busting through like we're not even there! They threw everything they had at us and we tried to hold them off, but you can't stop Panthers with thirty-calibers." Busi replied in a weakened voice and barely audible.

"Our artillery is slowing them, but it's just a matter of time…they'll be here before long. And they're not taking any prisoners." he continued.

"I'm sure you're right." the GI acknowledged.

The Sergeant laid his head back on the dirt and closed his eyes. He was so weak he could not move. The pain that ravaged his body was so bad he hoped his end would be soon. His head continued to pound and there was a ringing in his ears that was constant. He opened his eyes and looked down at his own mangled body. His jacket was torn and bloody, covered with mud. His pants were shredded and the bandage covering his leg wound was soaked in his blood. His boots were black with mud and had holes in them from shrapnel. His feet were so cold he couldn't feel them and his forty-five-caliber side arm was still holstered on his hip. He was a mess and thought that with any luck he would bleed to death and be dead by the time the enemy arrived.

Busi laid in the hole with his unfortunate companions for almost an hour... the only sounds were the moans of the men in the hole suffering from their wounds and the constant artillery shells flying overhead with some small arms fire. It all seemed to be getting closer. There was little movement in the hole as the doomed men contemplated their future and coped with their agony.

Busi thought about his mother and how much he would miss her. He smiled as his mind drifted back to his home. He could see his brothers and sisters running around their subsistence farm as young kids playing and having fun, even though they had nothing. He thought about the dirty coal- mining job he left with lousy pay and even less of a future. His thoughts now turned to sadness as he realized how miserable his twenty-four years of life had been up to now. Somehow, he thought, this seemed like a fitting end. The only consolation for him was that he would die in the service of his country and to him there was no greater honor.

He also thought about all the brave men in his squad that fought with him over his long journey. Davis, Sultzaberger, Wells, Harrigan, Popielarcheck, Hughes and even Peepsight...all dead or wounded. Then there was the First Squad with Wright, Bone and the rest...all dead and soon he would be among them.

His thoughts now shifted to what would happen as the German war machine rolled over his position. He hoped that his death would be quick and knew that the Germans would probably shoot all of them as they passed by their sanctuary. Totally helpless and no longer able to defend himself he accepted his fate. Although saddened, he welcomed the fact that he would no longer have to live in this misery. For six months now...no, for his whole life, he had never given up on anything, but this was his defining moment. He succumbed to the hopeless feeling that he could no longer go on.

The unmistakable sounds of advancing tanks filled the air and he opened his eyes one more time. He gathered enough strength to lean his upper body forward.

"Here they come boys. They're going to kill us all. Why don't we say a prayer together." Busi said sadly.

The men who could, sat up and bowed their heads.

"Our Father who art in heaven, hallowed be Thy name…" Busi led the others in the Our Father.

When the prayer ended, The Sergeant gathered enough energy to crawl up the side of the bomb crater, as the sounds of the tanks got closer. When he got to the top he looked toward the west where he expected to see the advancing German Army. He saw nothing. As he turned his head to the east, what he saw next astounded him. About two hundred yards approaching his position were six American Sherman tanks rumbling toward his position. Behind the tanks were several Jeeps and two ambulances. As he saw the red crosses on the approaching trucks a feeling of jubilation surged through his ravaged body. This was the happiest moment of his life!

"We're saved!! Busi screamed at his hole mates.

"The tanks are ours…and medics too." he continued.

He rolled over on his back and collapsed. The men in the hole cheered and shouted…a sense of euphoria came over them. A surge of adrenalin flowed through Busi's body and he climbed out of the hole and began waving his hands as several of the Shermans cruised by on their way to meet the enemy. An ambulance pulled up to the crater and two medics jumped from the cab and ran to the Sergeant. Busi collapsed on the ground as one medic knelt down next to him. The young medic looked at the blood stained uniform and mud soaked Sergeant and knew he was in bad shape.

"Hang on soldier, we got you now." the medic said reassuringly.

"Man, are we glad to see you." Busi replied.

The second medic headed for the hole and jumped in, disappearing from sight.

"There's a guy about a quarter of a mile straight toward the front. He's lying in a hole and he's in really bad shape. You guys gotta' get him…I promised him I would send help." Busi pleaded, not thinking of himself but of his wounded comrade.

The Medic quickly ran to the second ambulance and Busi could see him pointing in the direction of the wounded GI. The second ambulance took off bouncing through the snowy field and headed for the ill-fated soldier.

"Those guys will find him, don't worry." the medic said as he ran back and again knelt down next to Busi.

The Sergeant felt better knowing that someone was going after the badly injured GI.

Within a few minutes Busi was on a stretcher in the back of the ambulance. The medic sat next to the Sergeant as he began cleaning the holes in his hand and leg. Busi's crater mates were also secured in the truck and it began to speed away toward the rear.

"We've got to get the hell out of here. Those Shermans just happened by here and were looking for something to shoot at, so they headed for Rocherath." The medic said.

"We thought they were the Krauts. We're really catching hell. I don't think there's anyone left from my outfit." Busi informed the medic.

"The Krauts are punching through our lines and moving fast. We're trying to regroup on the Elsenborn Ridge but there's so much chaos it's been hard to get all the wounded back." the medic said.

The truck continued for about twenty minutes bouncing along the muddy Belgium roads and stopped at a large barn. The medics grabbed the stretcher and moved the Sergeant inside where there were many battered GIs from the Second Division. They laid him on a pile of hay and an Army doctor tended to his wounds. He was given a shot of Penicillin (the new antibiotic at that time), water and some k-rations. They did not stay long as the German Army continued its assault and continued to push the Americans back.

The brave medics and medical crew were unrelenting in their quest to get Busi and the rest of the battered GIs back to safety. They moved the GIs several times, each time stopping at safe points to tend to the wounded. After several hours of rough travel the ambulance came to a hospital and Busi realized that he was now back in France safe from the impending doom of the front lines.

As night fell on December 18th the Sergeant had survived, at least for now! In a small hospital somewhere in France, he was cleaned, bandaged and, for the first time in six months, slept in a bed with clean sheets. His pain was relieved somewhat by the medication he received, but his headache and nosebleeds continued through the night.

He lay in his bed that night and pondered his future and the future of the war. Would they patch him up and send him back to the front or was he finished as a combat soldier. How much longer would this war go on now that the Germans were revitalized? He thought about all the things he had done and seen over the past six months and shook his head in disbelief. No one would ever believe any of it. It was too horrible to even think about. It would be impossible for him to try to describe his experience to someone who was not there.

Reports kept coming in to the rear saying the German offensive continued. The Second Division would maintain a defensive position on December 19th at Elsenborn Ridge, Belgium that held firm against the German attack and eventually defeated the final Nazi spearhead.

It would take several months for the Allies to recover from what became known as the Battle of the Bulge. Eisenhower's plan to end the war by Christmas 1944 was shattered during the four days of December 16th through December 19th.

*The horrific battle that took place at the Lausdell Crossroads and the town of Rocherath took a tremendous toll on the Ninth Regiment. Six hundred soldiers made up the First Battalion, which included Companies A,B,C,D and K. Only ninety-seven men survived the onslaught. The entire Second Division (Ninth, Twenty-Third and Thirty-Eighth Regiments) suffered a total of over three thousand casualties in just four days.

The German toll was even greater. Over one hundred Panzer Division tanks were destroyed around the twin towns and estimates as high as five thousand, five hundred casualties…but the more staggering numbers were yet to come

From December 16th 1944 to January 28th 1945 (the demise of the German spearhead), the Americans had eight thousand four hundred ninety-seven dead, forty six thousand wounded, and twenty one thousand missing in action…over seventy five thousand casualties.

The German war machine was the big loser with twelve thousand, six hundred dead, fifty seven thousand wounded and fifty thousand captured…almost one hundred, twenty thousand casualties, all in four days.

On December 20, 1944 U.S. First Army Commanding General Hodges wrote to the troops of the Second Division:

"What the Second Infantry Division has done in the last four days will live forever in the history of the United States Army."

Sergeant Joseph Busi would lie in the small French hospital for over eight days and was eventually taken back to the shores of Normandy where his journey began. There he would stay for several weeks in an Army medical tent where surgeons tried, without success, to remove the shrapnel that had invaded his body at the Lausdell Crossroads.

In late January 1945, Busi was flown over the English Channel to an American Army hospital in London. He would spend many months receiving treatment for wounds he received at the Battle of the Bulge. His recovery would be long and painful.

NOTE: On December 31, 1944 reporter Harold Denny reported on, and The New York Times printed, a front page article entitled: "U.S. BATTALION'S STAND SAVES REGIMENT, DIVISION AND ARMY." Although there were some errors in his report, Denny describes in detail the many heroic actions of the Second Division. He mentions, by name, Lt. Col. William McKinley (great nephew of President William McKinley), Lt. Allyn Tedman, Sgt. Roberts and Sgt. Busi as well as many other men. He describes the role the Battalion played in averting a "disastrous defeat" in one of the greatest battles in American history." *N.Y Times, Dec. 30, 1944.*

*(Source: *Combat History of the Second Infantry Division in World War II, 1946).*

***Lausdell Crossroads – East of Rocherath, Belgium**
Farmhouse with destroyed barn in foreground. Destroyed enemy tanks visible.*
Artist – Tech Sergeant H. Standley – circa 1946.

U. S. Battalion's Stand Saves Regiment, Division and Army

By HAROLD DENNY
By Wireless to The New York Times

WITH AMERICAN FORCES, on the Western Front, Dec. 30— There is an old saying about the loss of a nail that caused the loss of a shoe that caused the loss of a horse and so on until this lost nail had lost a rider, a battle and a kingdom. A parallel to this, but in reverse, might be written out of the battle now raging on the American First Army's front.

By the gallantry of one battalion, a regiment was saved; by the fortitude of the regiment, a division was saved; and so on until the heroism of this one battalion had pyramided into a victorious defense at the precise point where the Germans had expected to break clear

ONE U. S. BATTALION SAVES WHOLE ARMY

Continued From Page 1

that they are adequate to any task. Under his leadership the battalion won its battle, though losing heavily out of its total front-line strength.

For three days and nights pre-

N.Y. Times Article December 31, 1944.
Article by Harold Denny, N.Y Times.

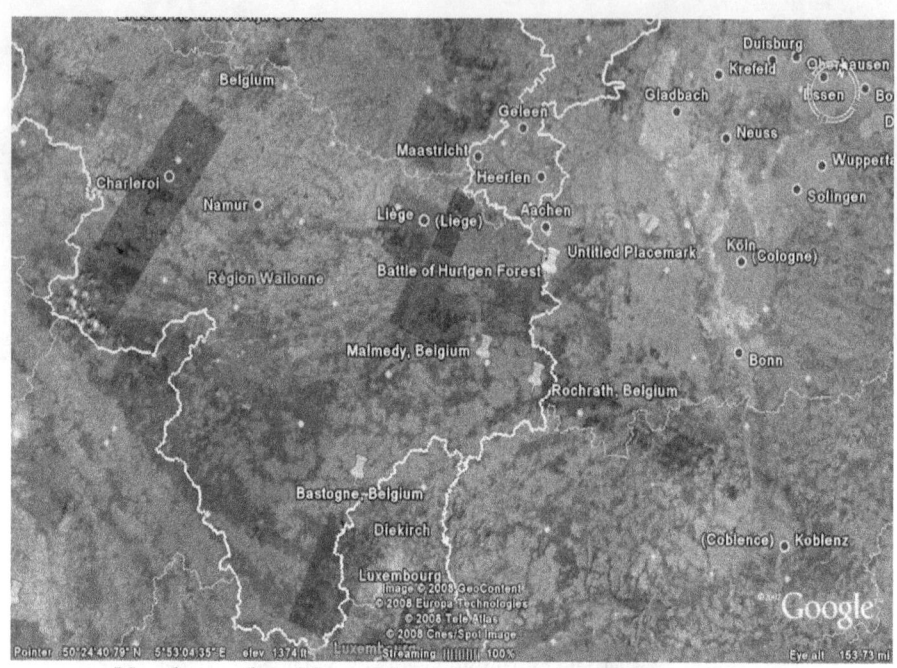

**Northern shoulder of the Battle of the Bulge –Rocherath, Belgium (near center of picture).
Famous town of Bastogne lower left.
German border visible right of Rocherath.
Luxembourg border visible right of Bastogne.
Hitler attacked across his border with twenty divisions (200,000 men) from Rocherath south to Luxembourg.**
Map by Google Earth

Chapter 13
V.E. Day and the Long Road Home
April 6th – June 23rd, 1945

"The surgeons had my leg cut open to tried and get the shrapnel out. They kept digging and digging with no anesthesia. Finally one doctor looked at his watch and tapped the other one on the shoulder as he was digging into my leg. He pointed to his watch and they both stopped the surgery. They immediately wrapped a bandage around my leg and told me they couldn't find the piece of shrapnel because it had moved. I was in agony. Then as they were leaving I asked them where they were going and they said they had to go to lunch. Just like that. I never saw those two doctors again." Sergeant Joseph Busi interview 2005.

For four long agonizing months Army doctors in London continued to work on Sergeant Busi. They tried on several occasions to remove the shrapnel in his hand and leg and also tried to shrink the blood clot in his brain. It took the Army so long to get him back to a decent hospital after he had been wounded, that the shrapnel in his body had moved and doctors could no longer find the metal. The blood clot in the frontal lobe of his brain was slowly dissolved by blood thinning medications but his headaches continued and nightly nosebleeds were a regular occurrence. He was again able to walk and the Army prepared him for travel.

On the morning of April 6, 1945 a nurse entered Joe's room with a big smile on her face.

"We're getting ready to move you, Sergeant." she said.

"They're sending me to the Pacific, aren't they?" he responded thinking he would be well enough to fight again.

"Are you kidding Sergeant? You're going home to stay. This war is over for you. You've done your duty." She replied.

Joe was ecstatic. He was going home. He couldn't believe it. He was sure the Army would be sending him to the unfinished business in the Pacific, but he was wrong.

After nineteen months on foreign soil, he would be returning to his Pennsylvania home and his family. It was beyond anything he could have imagined and he was amazed at the fact that he had survived.

By April 1945, there were rumors that the Germans were all but defeated and the collapse of the Third Reich was imminent as the Russians approached Berlin from the east. The Allies approached Berlin from the west but it would be the Russians that would first enter the city and claim victory over the Nazis.

On April 7, 1945 Sergeant Joseph Busi boarded an American transport ship and began his journey home. The ship would take seventeen days to cross the Atlantic and the Sergeant arrived in N.Y. Harbor on April 23rd. He was then transported to Camp Upton Convalescent Hospital (Yaphank, Long Island) where he continued his recuperation for the next two months.

On May 8, 1945 the war in Europe ended and Sergeant Busi rejoiced from his convalescence hospital with the entire nation that the Nazi Regime had been defeated.

On June 22, 1945, two years, nine months and four days after his induction, Joe Busi was given three hundred dollars mustering out pay, an honorable discharge and an unceremonious release from Camp Upton Hospital.

Joe hopped a train bound for Western Pennsylvania and his hometown of Saltsburg. Upon arriving Joe was reunited with his mother who he was convinced he would never see again, along with his brothers and sisters. It was one of the happiest days of his life and the family rejoiced for days.

Although Joe's heroics were a matter of record, his family was never told about what he had accomplished so many miles from home. Other than the national radio interview and recording, his family was unaware of Joe's six months in hell.

No one ever asked him questions and he never spoke of his ordeal until many years later. That was the way it was…no fanfare, no hoopla, and no pats on the back. He was expected to do his job, come home and resume his life as if nothing had ever happened…and that's exactly what he did!

Although Army Surgeons tried to remove the shrapnel that

tore into Joe's body on December 18th 1944 the shrapnel would never be surgically removed and the headaches from the blood clot in his brain continued for the next sixty plus years. The shrapnel in his right thumb moved to the second joint and today his thumb has limited movement.

Chapter 14
The Doughboy Returns
May 2nd – 5th, 2005 – Normandy, France

Our plans to visit Europe with my father included a trip to the Normandy Beaches, possibly west to Brest, Paris and on to Belgium, the site of the Battle of the Bulge. There would be a brief side trip to Luxembourg by invitation of the government for my father and my brother-in-law Jack Derevensky (First Army, First Division) to receive a decoration for the defense of their country during the Ardennes Offensive and Battle of the Bulge. Jack's service paralleled my father's, as he also landed in Normandy and fought through the end of the war. His wife, Marcelle, my wife, Paulette and my mother, Margaret rounded out our party on a trip that we will never forget. The six of us were in for an experience that was like none other.

    We looked forward with great anticipation to visiting the sites of World War II, but we had no idea what was in store for us as we departed the aircraft at DeGaulle Airport in Paris.

    The emotional roller coaster we were about to experience was unlike anything I had experienced in my previous fifty-three years.

    The ride from Paris to Normandy was rather mundane but shortly after arriving it occurred to me that this would not be an ordinary visit. We stayed at a quaint bed and breakfast in a nearby coastal town and the next morning we headed out for the beaches.

    As we approached "Bloody Omaha" I could see the anxiety all over my father's face as we exited the car and headed for the boardwalk. I was somewhat surprised by the monuments and sites that were clearly marked indicating the different landing sites of the Allies on December 6, 1944. We walked along the boardwalk until we came to a small plaque that read "Dog Red", the exact landing spot Sergeant Busi came ashore some sixty years earlier. We stopped and looked out toward the cold English Channel. Although some of the surroundings looked different to him, my father walked out on the sands of Bloody Omaha and stared at the water as if he were in a trance. With my mother at his arm I followed them out about half way to the shore. The tide was low, unlike D-Day 1944, but he stopped and looked at my mother and me.

"This is it. I can't believe I'm standing here today." he said as tears welled up in his eyes.

"I can't believe how many good men died here that day! What a terrible waste of life...all so young!" He continued.

Even after sixty-one years, as Joe stood on one of the bloodiest battlegrounds in human history, he thought not of his terrible pain and suffering that day, but that of his fallen comrades. I could only stare at the sea and try to imagine the death and destruction. As tears rolled down my cheeks I was unable to say anything. It was impossible for me to imagine the terror he must have felt as he came ashore on that miserable day sixty years ago. The scene was awe-inspiring.

The weather was terrible...cold, cloudy and windy, almost the exact conditions as D-Day. It was hard for any of us to speak. The thousands of questions I had about that day disappeared as I stood in awe on the solemn beach. After several minutes of silence we made our way back to the boardwalk.

Standing in front of the plaque marking Dog Red was a young couple with two small children who looked to be eight to ten years old. As we approached the family the young father, not more than thirty-five years old, noticed Joe's hat that I had purchased for him in the States. On the front it said "Second Division World War II" with the star and Indian head emblem. There were also several small replica "Hello! I noticed your hat. Were you here during the war?" he asked in perfect English with a slight Dutch accent.

"Yes, I landed here on D-Day." Joe replied.
The young man's eyes opened wide.

"Oh, I am honored to meet a true hero! We are from Holland and came here on vacation to visit the sites of the war. We are grateful for your sacrifice and I know that my family and me would not be standing here today had it not been for your courage." He said sincerely looking into Joe's eyes.

"We all know what happened here and I can tell you that we

are truly thankful for what you have done!" he continued as he reached out and shook Joe's hand.

I was flabbergasted. It occurred to me that this young Dutch family was more aware and appreciative of the sacrifices made by these brave men than many people in our own country.

We talked to the Dutch family for a few more minutes as both the husband and wife continued with their accolades. My father did not expect this type of reception and was his usual humble self, downplaying the heroics. The young father briefly explained to his two young daughters that Joe was at the beach on D-Day and told his girls to thank the brave American who came a great distance to save their country from the Nazis.

The girls looked up at Joe and respectfully thanked the old Sergeant. I could again see the tears well up in my father's eyes as he replied in kind. Until this day, he had never fully realized the impact he made, sixty years ago, on the lives of people like this young Dutch family. The gratitude of the family somehow made it all seem worth it to him. The family said their goodbyes and moved on to other parts of the beach.

We moved off the beaches and made our way up the St. Laurent draw where there were several World War II Museums. These Museums were dedicated to the Allied Soldiers and displayed the many weapons used during the invasion. As my father and I walked outside of one of the museums to look at a large artillery cannon, another young Dutch father, carrying a large book, and his teenage daughter approached us as we stood next to the huge gun.

"Excuse me sir, but I noticed your hat and I was wondering if you here during D-Day 1944?" The young man asked my father in perfect English.

"Yes I was. I was attached to the First Infantry Division and landed at Omaha Beach on D- Day." Joe replied for the second time in the same day.

" I am a history teacher from Holland and I am here with a large group of students and my daughter to visit World War II sites. It is truly an honor to meet a man of such courage!" He continued.

He pulled out the book from under his arm and presented it

to my father. He opened to a page where there were several pictures of D-Day and some writing under the pictures.

"We have put together this history book of what happened here and it would honor us greatly if you were to autograph this page…you are a true hero and we thank you for your bravery and sacrifice! What you men did here was truly amazing and should never be forgotten!" The young teacher said with great respect and humility.

Joe took the book and signed his name, rank and outfit along with date of his historic landing.

The man and his daughter stood next to Joe for fifteen minutes asking him questions about D-Day and other events of the war that he had experienced. The teenage daughter and her father listened intently to every word my father spoke. It was humbling for me to watch as the old Sergeant recalled moments of the war and answered their questions. The man and his daughter finished questioning Joe and again thanked him for his service. As they left the lot I could see the man relay his experience to the rest of his group as he pointed toward us.

We continued our first day tour ending up at Point du Hoc where the Army Rangers had mounted their assault on the one hundred foot cliffs. The summit of the Point was an overwhelming sight as the remnants of the Nazi bunkers and countless bomb craters lay undisturbed as they did sixty years ago.

My father began speaking again of that day and how he stood on his ship's deck and watched as the smoke billowed from the shore along these steep cliffs. He remembered he was to back up the Rangers that day but was sent instead to Dog Red.

We moved from bunker to bunker, incredulous at the massive structures built by the Nazis and it was impossible to imagine the battle that took place there years earlier.

Point du Hoc was a powerful reminder of the once mighty German war machine and the pain and suffering it inflicted on the invading Allies.

We spent several hours at the Point and at the end of an exhausting day our emotions ran high. For me the day was by far one of the most inspiring and profound events of my life. For my father it was a flash back to one of the worst days of his life. At eighty-six years old the experience was so overwhelming for him that he said very little. The stress and anxiety written on his face said volumes about what he had witnessed that day so many years ago.

The experience was emotionally draining for all of us, but it was nothing compared to what we would transpire the following day.

Day two of our trip included a visit to the American Cemetery at the beaches of Normandy. What happened on this day was so emotional and inspiring that I worried my eighty-six year-old father's health would be affected by the day's events.

We arrived at the cemetery early morning and entered the main building that housed many artifacts and information about the cemetery. My father and Jack would not be able to walk the entire area, so we procured a wheel chair for them to share.

I asked my father if there was one particular gravesite that he most wanted to visit and he immediately gave me the name of Private Robert Sultzaberger, his long time friend from boot camp who was killed in hedgerow country. Inside the large building was an older gentleman who manned a small desk with a computer. After giving him Sultzaberger's name, he instructed us to the gravesite.

As we left the building and approached the cemetery I could see the entrance gates and what lay beyond. What I saw was incredible. As far as the eye could see were rows and rows of beautiful white crosses and Jewish Stars all aligned in perfect order. The monuments stretched from the entrance gates north to the edge of the tree-lined bluffs directly above Bloody Omaha. We entered the gates and continued toward a huge cement structure several hundred yards inside the gates. There stood a memorial to all the brave American Soldiers who had paid the ultimate price for freedom. After reading all the memorials we made our way to find Robert Sultzaberger's grave and headed toward the center of the massive graveyard.

Two eight-foot concrete sidewalks on the edges of a thirty-foot grass center strip led us for two hundred yards to the center of the cemetery. Walking down the long sidewalk I looked in all directions. The only thing visible was the perfectly manicured green grass and the white monuments...thousands of them! It was the most humbling sight I have ever seen. It was hard for any of us to speak. I stopped and read some of the names and dates on the crosses.

"Some of these guys never saw their nineteenth birthday! What a shame. I could have easily been one of them, too." My father said in sad voice as he shook his head.

"I know dad...I'm glad you made it!" I replied as I patted him on the back.

In the exact center of the cemetery was a small round concrete chapel with several benches and a circular sitting area. Inside the chapel was a beautiful stained glass ceiling depicting the battle that took place just over the bluffs and a tribute to the fallen soldiers.

After silently observing the chapel for a few minutes I pushed my father in his wheelchair over to the row and grave number for Robert Sultzaberger. The site was just about twenty rows from the center chapel. I parked the chair next to the beautiful white cross with the inscription that said: "PVT Robert Sultzaberger – July 27,1944 – Pennsylvania." I looked at my father and I could see that it was almost too much for him to bear. He rose up out of his chair, put his hand on the cross and gave it a few taps as he lowered his head. His chin began to quiver and tears welled up in the old Sergeant's eyes.

"I'm so sorry, Sultz" He said as he shook his head side to side.

To this day I don't know whether my father was sad at the death of his friend or apologizing for the fact that he had survived. If I had to guess I think it was a little of both. Neither of us spoke another word.

I put my arm around the battle hardened Sergeant and we were both reduced to tears. I never knew Sultzaberger but it didn't matter. The sorrow was overpowering.

We composed ourselves and made our way back to the center chapel where the rest of the family was waiting. We were resting at the chapel area for a few minutes when I noticed a large group of twenty to twenty-five middle-aged women walking toward the chapel and us.

When they arrived they paid their respects at the chapel and began milling around in front of us. I spoke to one of the lovely women and found out that they had come from Dublin, Ireland. They were in France to tour the sites of WWII and chartered a bus to the American Cemetery.

One of the women noticed my father and Jack sitting on one of the benches. She looked at Joe's hat and took a step closer for a better look.

"Oh my lord, were you here on D-Day?" she asked Joe with a very noticeable Irish accent.

"Yes, right down there on that beach." my father said as he pointed toward the end of the bluffs and the English Channel.

The rest of the Irish Ladies, hearing the conversation, converged on the two World War II Veterans as if they were movie stars.

"I can't believe it. We are so privileged to meet you!" another women yelled out as they surrounded the two doughboys.

Joe and Jack stood up and several other parties joined the group of Irish tourists. There were now over thirty people surrounding the two heroes and the questions began to fly.

"What was it like?" asked another women.

"I don't think I can describe it, but it was pretty bad." Jack answered.

"You men are real heroes and we cannot thank you enough!" she replied.

"No, the real heroes are still here… in this place, they never made it home!" my father replied as he lowered his head.

Suddenly there was silence. The women began to break out the tissues and several began sobbing. By now several other European Families had joined the Irish group and surrounded the two Americans. They began talking to them and many of the people there had family members take pictures with the two old soldiers. It was a love-fest that I never would have believed if I hadn't seen it with my own eyes.

The crowd continued to grow and get closer to the two celebrities. I could see that my father was becoming overwhelmed by it all. He began staring off into space and was almost unable to speak at times. I moved through the crowd and put my arm around him to see if he was all right. He looked at me...his eyes were the size of silver dollars, magnified by his thick glasses. I could see he was astonished by all the attention. I realized he was fine and just taking it all in. It was quite a sight. There was hugging and kissing, families taking pictures and in the middle of it all were two old American doughboys not really sure what this was all about.

A young Dutch family moved closer through the crowd toward my father for a picture. Their young daughter around four years old ran to him and wrapped her arms around his right leg and squeezed tightly.

"Thank you, thank you!" the little girl cried out as Joe looked down at the tiny girl strapped to his leg.

That was all Joe could take. His lower lip quivered again and tears began running down his cheek. I tried to hold back my tears but it was impossible as the crowd marveled at the two heroes. He put his arm around the girl and gave her a squeeze. The proud parents snapped a quick picture and the love fest continued.

One by one the Irish women made their way to the two old soldiers. Each one hugged and kissed the old boys thanking them profusely, as if it were V-E Day, 1945.

After answering a multitude of questions and taking hundreds of pictures the crowd began to disperse, but the Irish clan wasn't finished just yet.

All twenty-five of the beautiful older women circled the doughboys and joined their arms together. They began swaying back and forth and broke out into song. They sang a heart-felt version of "Oh Danny Boy" and there wasn't a dry eye within fifty feet of the congregation. Joe and Jack stood in the middle of the circle leaning on their canes with their heads down, crying like two little children. It was an amazing scene to witness!

When the song ended, the women again gave the soldiers one last hug and thanked them for their sacrifice. As quickly as they came they were gone. Joe and Jack sat on one of the concrete benches, totally exhausted trying to understand what had just happened. It took a few minutes for them to regain their composure.

This hour-long gathering was highly emotional and one of the most poignant moments of my life.

As we exited the cemetery we again passed hundreds of gravesites and the two old soldiers, overwhelmed by the day's events, agonized over the number of fallen soldiers. It was a humbling experience for everyone, but Joe and Jack knew more than anyone how lucky they were to have been able to live out their lives. The cemetery was a haunting reminder of the young men who never made it home…their young lives cut short sixty years earlier.
NOTE: The thousands of graves in Normandy represent only some of the casualties that occurred in just a few short months in Europe during 1944–1945. It is a sobering reminder of the price of our freedom and should be something every American should witness.

Sergeant Joseph Busi - Normandy Beaches - May 2005
Photo by Paulette Busi

Crowd gathers around D-Day Survivors Sergeant Joe Busi (with hat, right) and friend Jack Derevensky (1st Division), Normandy Cemetery - May 2005
Photo by Don Busi

Don Busi

Irish tourist thanks The Sergeant at Normandy Cemetery – 2005
Photo by Paulette Busi

Chapter 15
Pomp, Circumstance and One Bad Memory
May 12th–16th, 2005 - Luxembourg and Belgium

On a typical European mountain road on the outskirts of the small town of Vienden, Luxembourg our family gathered with several other families and dignitaries. There was a small monument on the side of the road with the names of fifty or sixty men of a brave outfit of American Engineers who saved the town in December 1944. This brave outfit of combat engineers held off the great German spearhead but paid a heavy price in casualties.

My father and Jack had been invited to participate in the ceremony to commemorate not only the men who saved Vienden, but all the former soldiers of the Battle of the Bulge and the Ardennes.

The ceremony lasted about forty-five minutes and was highlighted by a speech given by the U.S. Ambassador to Luxembourg. A U.S. Army color guard stood at attention as the names of the fallen were read and the twenty-five survivors stood on their canes and tried to hold back the tears.

When the ceremony was over twelve U.S. Army vehicles from WWII pulled up and loaded up the Veterans for a formal parade through the town and to the city center.

The parade wound down the mountain to the center street of Vienden as hordes of towns people lined the street and hung from their windows. They waved American flags and shouted at the old soldiers as if it was 1944 and they had just been liberated. It was an awesome sight.

The parade ended in the center of town at a large recreation center where the Veterans were treated to Champaign and orange juice. A U.S. Army Band played on the stage as the huge crowd of three hundred gathered in the large auditorium. The Vets were seated at the front of the auditorium with their families and the mayor then called up each individual.

Two uniformed Luxembourg Soldiers stood at attention and presented a large gold medal minted by the Luxembourg Government commemorating the Battle of the Ardennes. One by one they were called up by name to receive their honors. It was heart-wrenching as my eighty-five year old father walked with his cane to the front and stood at attention before the Luxembourg Soldier. The soldier placed the medal around his neck and saluted my father. My father dutifully returned the salute as the two soldiers showed the tremendous respect they had for each other.

One soldier was young and at the prime of his life while the other very near the end of his. Both men respectful o f each other's service to their country. I knew as I watched the exchange that the young man from Luxembourg was sincere in his respect for my father and the other Americans who sacrificed so much for their people of their country.

He knew as well as all the other people of Vienden that it was because of these brave men and the sacrifices they made we were able to celebrate this day. It showed on his face and the faces of every person in that town!

During our short stay in this lovely mountain town I was extremely proud to be an American. In some cases Europeans are not friendly to American visitors, but it was not the case this day. We were treated royally and the two old soldiers deserved everything they got. It was a magnificent day.

The next day would not be so glorious. We arose early in anticipation of finding the Lausdell Crossroad, just east of Rocherath, Belgium where my father and the valiant men of the Ninth fought one of the bloodiest battles of WWII.

It was a cold, rainy day and as we approached the town of Rocherath, my father began to mumble incoherently. He began mumbling about how we would never find the crossroad and even if we did he wouldn't recognize it. His mumbling continued as we drove out of town on a small paved road that took us east toward Germany. Suddenly, about a quarter of a mile out of town I stopped the car at a series of farm roads. As looked to my left as if something told me to look, I saw the farmhouse and the barn. We had some pictures of the crossroads that a soldier had sent my father while he was stationed in Germany during the 1980s. I looked at the photos and realized that this was the place.

"*This is it! The farmhouse, the barn, this is it!* I shouted.

There was silence. As I looked back at my father he was in a trance as if he wasn't there. He stared at the farmhouse as if he had seen a ghost. The crossroad lay to our right so I drove past the farmhouse and turned at the Lausdell Crossroads.

The roads had been paved and the area was quite innocuous. There was no one around and other than the barn being rebuilt and the roads paved nothing had changed since 1944. I could see the Krinkelt Forest and the centuries old hedges that lined the lonely country roads.

As we exited the car it began to rain and the cold damp air filtered right through our light jackets. It was may and I was freezing. I couldn't imagine how cold it must have been in December 1944. My father walked to the crossroads and had a confused look on his face and began again to mumble incoherently. He started babbling about how the hedges were not the same and the trees were different. I showed him the pictures of the farmhouse and it was an exact match. He rambled around for a few minutes and walked up toward the farmhouse and back. The wind began to blow and I could hardly stand the cold, but the old doughboy didn't feel a thing. After a few confusing minutes he realized that this was the place and it was horrifying for him. He began to babble again and wanted to walk the quarter mile to the rear where Popielarcheck was killed. My wife and I looked at each other with worried faces. We were both concerned about his well-being.

I convinced him to get into the car and drive to the spot, but I was more concerned about the effects of this visit. I couldn't help but think that this was devastating for him and quite overwhelming. I drove back to the spot where he tried so desperately to save Pop's life and before the car came to a halt he opened the front door and almost fell out of the moving car. I knew then that this was too much for one afternoon. We all got out and he tried to explain how it all happened but it became too much. He showed us the hedgerow where he and Popielarcheck had been hit by the eight-eight millimeter shell. He even knew the exact spot where the shell exploded.

He was extremely emotional and I knew it was time to go. I used the weather as an excuse to leave and told him we could come back the next day. We all agreed and left without any further anxiety.

Now that my father had seen the dreadful spot where he came so close to death, I thought it would be best to let it all sink in and come back the next day. I was right.

Although he didn't sleep one minute that night, the next day when we returned I could see he was more composed then the day before as if he come to grips with what had happened at the crossroads.

The weather had turned sunny and when we arrived my father began to calmly explain everything. As he spoke I could imagine the German Tanks and thousands of enemy soldiers converging on that very spot. It was fascinating to see the actual location of this great battle and to be with someone who had experienced it all.

We moved along the road past the farmhouse to the spot where my father had been wounded and Popielarcheck lost his life. We walked along the hedge that concealed the two men until the fatal shell hit Pop and changed my father's life forever. It was quite emotional as he showed the exact spot of the incident and how close the enemy was to him. It was one bad memory for the old Sergeant and it showed on his face. Not much was said after that and as I walked the area of the Lausdell Crossroads I realized that anyone passing through this innocent looking area would never know what happened here. Thousands of men lost their lives in the area yet not one sign of the struggle existed.

Trees had been planted, the barn had been rebuilt, roads were paved and hundreds of cattle roamed the hedge-lined fields as if it had been that way for thousands of years. The peaceful and quiet Belgium countryside gave no indication of the death and destruction that occurred there so many years ago. I had an eerie feeling and I felt as if I were walking on solemn ground.

We stayed for hours roaming the countryside with my father as he explained each detail of the battle as if it had happened yesterday. He meticulously pointed out where his machine gun placements were located and where his close friend "Peepsight" had been blown to pieces by yet another shell from a German Panther Tank. As it is with many of our remaining veterans of WWII dementia has crept into his mind, but recollections of the war are as lucid to him as if it just happened. I took it all in and it was fascinating.

As we left the Lausdell Crossroads I heard my father comment that he was glad he had come back after all these years. I got a sense from him that maybe now that he had come back it would be easier for him to come to terms with what happened to him so many years ago. I'm not sure if I was correct in my assertion.

We visited many other towns in Belgium including Malmady (site of the Malmedy Massacre), Stavalot and Spa, but none made the impact on my father like the visit to the Lausdell Crossroads in Rocherath. It is the spot where he confronted the most significant event that a human being can experience…his own mortality. With the certain deaths of so many of his friends and his own death imminent, it would be impossible for him to remain unchanged.

After returning home, my father made the comment that the trip to Europe was truly overwhelming for him and it seemed almost like a dream. He continues to talk about the trip and even admits he would like to go back again, but I fear his age will not permit it.

My purpose for the trip was for the old Sergeant to see what has transpired in the places he had been and also to see the impact his sacrifices have made on some of the people in Europe. The people of Europe we spoke with seemed to be very aware of what happened there sixty-one years earlier and they openly showed their appreciation.

We saw the prosperity and talked to the people, but it did nothing to ease my father's mind or quell his survival guilt. It is a weight that he will carry with him until the day he dies.

Afterword

The three years that Joe spent in the U.S. Army and in particular the six plus months in combat, made the most profound impact on his life. He was never the same again. The horrors of what he had seen and done continue to haunt Joe until today. The scenes of death and destruction are as real to him today as they were sixty years ago and are played out in his mind on a daily basis.

The guilt of his survival has haunted him for all these years. The question he has asked himself thousands of times: "Why did I survive and the others didn't?" remains unanswered. It is a question that cannot be answered yet he continues to search for an explanation. It has been his faith in God (that a higher power had intervened in his survival) that has given him some solace throughout the years. Along with his war injuries, his guilt and anxiety remain, even today. Those feelings were evident on his return to Europe in 2005, sixty-one years later.

After his release from the Army in 1945, Joe suffered from nosebleeds, headaches and some loss of movement in his thumb from the shrapnel. Although some of the physical effects have subsided his sleepless nights and headaches continue to this day. The mental anguish he suffers from also continues. There was no psychiatric help from the U.S. Army in 1945 and many soldiers with emotional scars were left to their own devices. If a soldier was to ask for psychiatric help it would go on his permanent record and getting a job would be virtually impossible. No one would ever hire a "psycho."

After the war, Joe went home and tried to pick up his life where he left off years before. Although he went on to raise a family and tried to live a normal life, the horrors of those six months in Europe during 1944 have been with him every day. They will haunt him until the day he dies.

Private First Class Wells, Joe's number two gunner in the beginning of the war, wrote to Joe after the war to tell him he had survived the bullet wound to his head. Joe found out later that soon after the letter was written, Wells died. He died from complications from his wound that he received in hedgerow country.

Joe also was informed that Private Dock Snyder who was reassigned from the Second Squad shortly after the Battle of Brest was killed on February 9, 1945 when the Second Division again crossed the west wall of the Siegfried Line. In the final count, out of the eight men in the Second Squad and the nine men of the First Squad, Sergeant Joe Busi, Pvt. Ed Rothenberry (lost at the Battle of Brest and reassigned) and Pvt. Red Clayton were the only three survivors of the War.

It is impossible for any of us to understand what it was like for my father during those dark days in Europe, and even harder to know what it has been like for him to carry around those horrific memories every day since.

In the town of Rocherath, Belgium, there is a small city park located in the middle of town with several beautiful monuments to the men who fought and died in the area during the Battle of the Bulge. On one such monument there is an inscription written in English, German, French and Dutch. The inscription is incredibly profound and describes the sentiments of my father and the other brave soldiers who fought in World War II.

The inscription reads: *"May God help you to understand what the fighting here and in the area was like, for there was such a distance between those who suffered and those who observed suffering from afar."*

Only those who were there will ever know what it was like.

It is astonishing to me how the brave warriors of the WWII generation downplay what they did in Europe and in the Pacific. It is as if what they did was routine and ordinary, yet what this group of brave soldiers did was quite extraordinary. They saved the world. They saved the world from a maniacal lunatic that, given the chance, could have inflicted even more unimaginable horrors on mankind.

Adolf Hitler was evil and there will be more Hitlers to come. The only way we can prevent Hitler's brand of evil in the future is to remember what happened. Hitler's brand of evil, as repulsive as it was, must be remembered by every generation for as long as our country survives. If what these brave men did is forgotten then we have only ourselves to blame when another tyrant rises up and inflicts untold atrocities on the human race. We must remember how and why evil was allowed to flourish and we must never forget the courageous soldiers who defeated it.

References
1. Army & Navy Publishing Company, *Combat History of the Second Infantry Division in World War II,* 1946.
2. Barnes and Noble Books, *U.S. Army Atlas of the European Theater in World War II,* 2004.
3. Denny, Harold, "U.S. Battalion's Stand Saves Regiment, Division and Army." *New York Times,* December 31, 1944, Front Page.
4. Editors of Time, ""D-Day – 24 Hours That Saved The World." *Time Books,* 2004.
5. MacDonald, Charles B., *A Time For Trumpets,* (Wm Morrow Publishing, 1985).
6. Pimlott, John, *Battle Of The Bulge.* (Gallery Books, 1981).
7. National Archives, "The German Breakthrough (V Corps Sector.)" Interview: Maj. William F. Hancock. S/Sgt. Norman Bernstein. 1st Battalion, 9th Infantry, 2nd Infantry Division, March 17, 1945.
8. National Archives, "B Company Engagement East of Rocherath, Belgium. Lt. Roy Allen, December 18, 1944.
9. Stars and Stripes, *From D+1 to 105. Story of the 2nd Infantry Division,* Paris 1944-1945.
10. The Bulge Bugle, "Veterans of the Battle of the Bulge." George Chekan – Editor, May 2006.
11. Whitehead II, Alfred T. "Diary of a Soldier." Chapter 7b, Chapter 10b, http://home.thirdage.com/Military/friends2idww2/10b-Whitehead.html

Glossary

A

Air Corp.- The **United States Army Air Corps** (USAAC) was the predecessor of the United States Army Air Force (USAAF) from 1926 to 1941, which in turn was the forerunner of today's United States Air Force (USAF).

Ammo- Ammunition, often referred to as **ammo**, is a generic term meaning (the assembly of) a projectile and its propellant.

Ammo Belt - A **belt** is a device that holds cartridges adjacent to each other in a single row for feeding into a firearm.

Ardennes - The **Ardennes** is a region of extensive forests and rolling hill country, primarily in Belgium and Luxembourg, but stretching into France.

B

Bronze Star - A United States Armed Forces individual military decoration which may be awarded for bravery, acts of merit, or meritorious service. When awarded for bravery, it is the fourth-highest combat award of the U.S. Armed Forces and the 9th highest military award (including both combat and non -combat awards) in the order of precedence of U.S. military decorations.

Burp Gun - The **MP40** ("machine pistol 40") is a submachine gun developed in Germany and used extensively by paratroopers and platoon and squad leaders, and other troops during World War II. It fired up to 500 rounds per minute.

C

Command Post - A military term referring to a field Military communications location whence the person in charge of a situation may issue orders. Command posts are typically temporary and are located to allow maximum access to the site or battlefield with minimal risk to the person in charge.

Corporal - A rank in use in some form by most militaries, police forces or other uniformed organizations around the world. Corporal is a non-commissioned officer and may direct the activities of other soldiers. **Corporal (CPL)** is preceded by the first three forms of Private and the rank of Specialist. A Corporal ranks above a Specialist and below a Sergeant, but shares the same pay grade.

D

D-Day - A term often used in military parlance to denote the day on which a combat attack or operation is to be initiated. "D-Day" often represents a variable, designating the day upon which some significant event will occur or has occurred. The initial *D* in D-Day has had various meanings in the past, while more recently it has obtained the connotation of "Day" itself, thereby creating the phrase "Day-Day", or "Day of Days".

Division - A unit typically consisting of between 10,000 to 20,000 troops.

Dog Red – Code name for one of eight smaller beaches making up the larger landing beachhead known as Omaha Beach.

E

Eighty-Eight Millimeter Artillery - An anti-aircraft and anti-tank artillery gun from World War II. They were widely used throughout the war, and could be found on almost every battlefield. Developments of the original models led to a wide variety of guns that could be identified as "an 88".

F

Fatherland - The English word is now associated with the Nazi government of Germany (unlike in Germany itself, where the word means simply "homeland").

Foxhole - A defensive fighting position of several types of earthwork constructed in a military context. A DFP (known more commonly as a "**foxhole**" (U.S. military slang), generally refers to a position large enough to accommodate a soldier's entire body and equipment.

G

Geneva Convetions - Consist of four treaties formulated in Geneva, Switzerland, that set the standards for international law for humanitarian concerns. They chiefly concern the treatment of non-combatants and prisoners of war. They do not affect the use of weapons in war, which are covered by the Hague Conventions of 1899 and 1907.

G.I. - A term describing a member of the US armed forces or an item of their equipment. It may be used as an adjective or as a noun. The term is often thought to be an initialism of "Government Issue" but the origin of the term is in fact *galvanized iron* after the letters

"GI" that used to denote equipment such as metal trash cans made from it in U.S. Army inventories and supply records.

H

Hedgehog - A static obstacle defense made of angle iron(that is, lengths with an L- or I- shaped cross section) deployed during World War II by various combatants.

Hedgerow - A line of closely spaced shrubs and bushes, planted and trained in such a way as to form a barrier or to mark the boundary of an area. In France, usually planted on top of a small mound of dirt to further solidify the boundary.

Higgins Boat - A landing craft used extensively in World War II. The craft was designed by Andrew Higgins of Louisiana, based on boats made for operating in swamps and marshes. More than 20,000 were built, by Higgins Industries and licensees. Also known as the **Landing Craft, Vehicle, Personnel (LCVP).**

M

M-1 or M-1 Gerand - The first semi-automatic rifle to be generally issued to the infantry in any nation. The rifle's ability to rapidly fire powerful .30-06 rifle ammunition also proved to be of considerable advantage in combat.

M1917A1 Browning Water Cooled Machine Gun – Fully automatic, recoil operated, water cooled weapon designated as a Heavy Machine Gun. It was not a weapon easily used in fluid combat or assault. However, the weight of this water-cooled weapon also gave it great stability, which, with its capability of sustained volume of fire, made it an excellent defensive weapon.

Malmedy Massacre - Refers to a war crime in which unarmed American prisoners of war were executed by their German captors. The massacre was committed on December 17, 1944 by Kampfgruppe Peiper (part of the 1st SS Panzer Division), a German combat unit, during the Battle of the Bulge.

Medic - A military member trained in battlefield medicine.

Messerschmitt - A famous German aircraft manufacturer, known primarily for its World War II
fighter aircraft, notably the Bf 109 and Me 262.

Mortar – A weapon that fires shells at a much lower velocity and higher ballistic arc than other ordnance; their shells explode on impact with target.

N

Normandy - A geographical region that is situated along the coast of France south of the English Channel between Brittany (to the west) and Picardy (to the east) and comprises territory in northern France and the Channel Islands.

O

Oak Leaf Cluster - A common device which is placed on U.S. military awards and decorations to denote those who have received more than one bestowal of a particular decoration. The number of oak leaf clusters typically indicates the number of subsequent awards of the decoration.

Omaha Beach - The code name for one of the principal landing points of the Allied invasion of German-occupied France in the Normandy landings on June 6, 1944, during World War II. The beach was located on the northern coast of France, facing the English Channel, and was 5 miles (8 km) long, from east of Sainte-Honorine-des-Pertes to west of Vierville-sur-Mer.

P

Panther or Panzer Tank - A tank fielded by Germany in World War II that served from mid-1943 to the end of the European war in 1945. It was intended as a counter to the T-34, and to replace the Panzer IV and III, though it served along with them and the heavy tanks until the end of the war. The Panther's excellent combination of firepower, mobility, and protection served as a benchmark for other nations' late war and immediate post-war tank designs.

Patrol - A small tactical grouping sent out by land, sea or air to perform a specific task. A patrol may be a reconnaissance patrol, sent to investigate some feature of interest, or a **fighting patrol** (US **combat patrol**), sent to find and engage the enemy.

Pillbox - Military term for a type of bunker.

Platoon - A military unit, typically composed of two to four sections or squads and containing about 30 to 50 soldiers.

P.O.W. – Military term for "Prisoner of War."

Private - A soldier of the lowest military rank. In the U.S. Army, **Private (PVT)** is used for the two lowest enlisted ranks, just below Private First Class.

P.F.C. or Private First Class - The third lowest enlisted rank, just above Private and below Corporal or Specialist in the Army. Usually represented by displaying one stripe on uniform.

Prohibition - Known as *Dry Law*, refers to a sumptuary law in a given jurisdiction which prohibits alcohol. Typically, the manufacture, transportation, import, export, and sale of alcoholic beverages is restricted or illegal. The term often refers specifically to the period from 1920 to 1933, during which alcohol sale, manufacture and transportation were banned throughout the United States.

Purple Heart - A United States military decoration awarded in the name of the President to those who have been wounded or killed while serving on or after 5 April 1917 with the U.S. military.

R

Regiment - A military unit, composed of a variable number of battalions - commanded by a colonel. It ranges in size from a few hundred to 5,000 soldiers (3 to 7 standard companies). Generally, regiments are grouped as divisions as in the Second Infantry Division which was comprised of the Ninth, Twenty-Third and Thirty-Eighth Infantry Regiments during World War II.

S

SS Troops - The combat arm of the *Schutzstaffel* ("Protective Squadron") or SS. In contrast to the Wehrmacht, Germany's regular army, the Waffen-SS was an elite combat unit composed of volunteer troops with particularly strong personal commitments to Nazi ideology. The origins of the Waffen-SS can be traced back to the creation of a group of 322 men who were to act as Hitler's bodyguard.

Sergeant - A rank used in some form by most militaries, police forces, and other uniformed organizations around the world. There are several ranks of sergeant, the lowest carries the title of **Sergeant (SGT)**, colloquially referred to as *buck sergeant* (A new sergeant within one year). Sergeant is the fifth enlisted rank in the U.S. Army, just above Specialist and Corporal and below Staff Sergeant, and is the second-lowest grade of non-commissioned officer. Sergeants typically command team-sized elements. Usually represented by displaying three stripes on uniform.

Sherman Tank - The primary tank produced by the United States for its own use and the use of its Allies during World War II.

Shrapnel - The term commonly used to describe the metal fragments and debris thrown out by any exploding object, be it a high explosive (HE) filled shell or a homemade bomb wrapped with nails or ball bearings.

Siegfried Line - A defense system stretching more than 630km (392 miles) with more than 18,000 bunkers, tunnels and tank traps. It went from Kleve on the border with the Netherlands, along the western border of the old German Empire as far as the town of Weil am Rhein on the border to Switzerland. Adolf Hitler planned the line from 1936 and had it built between 1938 and 1940.

Silver Star - The fourth highest military decoration that can be awarded to a member of any branch of the United States Armed Forces. It is also the third highest award given for valor (in the face of the enemy). It may be awarded to any person who, while serving in any capacity with the U.S Armed Forces, distinguishes him or herself by extraordinary heroism.

S.O.P. – Abbreviation for "Standard Operating Procedure." Used to describe a procedure or set of procedures to perform a given operation or evolution or in reaction to a given event.

T

Thirty-Caliber – Reference to the M1917A1 water cooled machine gun which used 30 caliber ammunition.

Tree Bursts – German artillery fire that was fused to detonate as the shell struck the tops of the conifer trees of the Hurtgen Forest, Belgium during World War II. As the shell dotonated, a deadly spray of shrapnel and tree fragments rained down on the enemy (mostly American GIs positioned in the forest).

Trench Foot - A medical condition caused by prolonged exposure of the feet to damp, unsanitary and cold conditions above freezing point. Also known as "Immersion Foot."

Turret - A device that protects the crew or mechanism of a projectile firing weapon and at the same time lets the weapon be aimed and fired in many directions. In modern tanks the turret is armored for crew protection and rotates a full 360 degrees carrying a single large-caliber tank gun. In modern tanks the turret is armoured for crew protection and rotates a full 360 degrees carrying a single large-calibre tank gun.

V

V.E. Day – Abbreviation for "Victory in Europe Day."

www.ingramcontent.com/pod-product-compliance
Lightning Source LLC
Chambersburg PA
CBHW061651040426
42446CB00010B/1684